GREAT CITIES

THROUGH THE AGES

NEW YORK

Erratum
On page 5 the date of September 11, 2002
should read September 11, 2001.
We regret the error.

First American Edition published in 2003
by Enchanted Lion Books
115 West 18 Street, New York, NY 10011

Library of Congress Cataloging-in-Publication Data

Weber, Paige.
New York / Paige Weber. — 1st American ed.
p. cm — (Great cities through the ages)
Includes index.
Produced by McRae Books
Summary: Illustrations and text provide an overview of the history of New York City, from its founding by the Dutch in the 1600s to the present day.

ISBN 1-59270-003-9

1. New York (N.Y.)—History—Juvenile literature. [1. New York (N.Y.)—History.] I. McRae Books. II Title. III. Series.
F128.33.W43 2003
974.7'1—dc21   2003040793

Printed and bound in Belgium
1 2 3 4 5 / 09 08 07 06 05 04 03

McRae Books Srl
Borgo S. Croce, 8, 50122 — Florence, Italy
info@mcraebooks.com

Text: Paige Weber
Illustrations: Andrea Ricciardi di Gaudesi, Studio Stalio (Alessandro Cantucci, Fabiano Fabbrucci, Andrea Morandi, Ivan Stalio), Lorenzo Cecchi, Lucia Mattioli, Paola Ravaglia, Antina Breithaupt, Gian Paolo Faleschini
Graphic Design: Marco Nardi
Layout: Sebastiano Ranchetti
Editors: Claire Moore, Anne McRae
Picture Research: Claire Moore, Loredana Agosta, Paige Weber, Andrea Ricciardi di Gaudesi
Cutouts: Filippo Delle Monache, Alman Graphic Design
Color Separations: Litocolor, Florence (Italy)

ACKNOWLEDGEMENTS
All efforts have been made to obtain and provide compensation for the copyright to the photos and artworks in this book in accordance with legal provisions. Persons who may nevertheless still have claims are requested to contact the copyright owners.

t=top; tl=top left; tc=top center; tr=top right; c=center; cl=center left; cr=center right; b= bottom; bl=bottom left; bc=bottom center; br=bottom right

6–7c A detail of a Map of New Amsterdam, 1660 "The Castello Plan", Museum of the City of New York, The J. Clarence Davies Collection, 29.100.709; 8t Ratzer, Bernard. Plan of the City of New York, surveyed in 1766 & 1767. London, 1776, The New York Public Library; 9t Southeast Prospect of the City of New York, Accession number 1904.1, Collection of The New York Historical Society; 10c Library of Congress, Prints and Photographs Division [G3804.N4.1811.B7]; 10–11bc Tontine Coffee House, Accession number 1907.32, Collection of The New York Historical Society; 14cr New York City subway map © Metropolitan Transportation Authority. Used with permission; 16cl James H. Cafferty and Charles G. Rosenburg, Wall Street, Half past 2 o'clock, October 13, 1857, The Panic of 1857, Wall Street 1857, Museum of the City of New York, Gift of the Hon. Irwin Untermyer, 40.54; 18c © Lee Ross, Sky View Pictures; 20br Court at No. 24 Baxter St. ca. 1890, Museum of the City of New York, The Jacob A. Riis Collection, #108, 90.13.4.111; 22tr The Granger Collection, New York; 22tl Library of Congress, Prints and Photographs Division [LC-USZ62-11202]; 23cl Library of Congress, Prints and Photographs Division [LC-BZ-80-3]; 24c Edward Hopper, American, 1882–1967, Nighthawks, 1942, oil on canvas, 84.1 x 152.4 cm, Friends of American Art Collection, 1942.51, © The Art Institute of Chicago; 25cl Jessie Tarbox Beals, Polly's Restaurant, Photograph of Greenwich Village Postcard, Museum of the City of New York, 91.53.5; 29br Alfred Eisenstaedt/Timepix; 30–31bc Farabola Foto (The Bridgeman Art Library); 32b Courtesy of the Queens Borough Public Library, Long Island Division, Frederick W. Weber Collection; 40tc Associated Press; 40cl Bonfire of the Vanities: The Kobal Collection/Warner Bros/Louis Goldman; 42cr Superman IV: The Kobal Collection/Cannon/DC Comics/David James, 42b Batman: The Kobal Collection/20th Century Fox/Greenway; 43c John Bachmann, A detail of New York City and Environs, Printed by C. Fatzer, Publisher: John Bachmann, 1859, Museum of the City of New York, Gift of James Duane Taylor, 31.24.

The Publishers would also like to thank the following photographers and picture libraries for the photos used in this book.
Corbis/Contrasto: 30tr; Corbis/De Bellis: 40cr; Corbis/Grazia Neri: 23t, 25t, 26cl, 37bl, 39c, 39tr, 39bc, 40cl, 43tc, 43bc, 43br; Eve Deacon: 15cr, 23bc; Lonely Planet Images: 15b Kim Grant, 25bl Kim Grant; Loredana Agosta: 33cl; Marco Nardi: 10tr, 15tc, 15br, 18bl, 21bl, 22br, 23br, 25br, 35tc, 36bl, 36–37c, 37tl, 37tr, 37cr, 38tl, 41tl, 41br, 42br ; The Image Works: 15cl, 26c, 28cr, 31br, 33tr, 33b, 35c, 38br, 40b, 41tc, 41tr, 43bl. "Theme from NEW YORK, NEW YORK" (John Kander, Fred Ebb) © reprinted by permission of Warner Bros. Publications 43tr.

GREAT CITIES THROUGH THE AGES

NEW YORK

Paige Weber

ENCHANTED LION BOOKS
New York

New York's movement of Abstract Expressionism was led by Jackson Pollock (1912–56) and his action painting.

Before the arrival of Dutch settlers in New York, at least six different tribes linked through language and culture lived in the area. They called themselves the Lenape, or "real men." They fished, hunted, and cultivated the "Three Sisters" — corn, beans, and squash. They wore tanned animal skins, and bear and beaver fur in winter. They told stories, but had no written language. One of the many footpaths they used was an important north-south trail on Manhattan which eventually became modern Broadway (right).

Table of Contents

The Roman Catholic St. Patrick's Cathedral on Fifth Avenue, consecrated in 1879, was built in Gothic style and its spires rise 330 feet from the ground.

NEW YORK

1625 The first permanent settlement of lower Manhattan is made.

1638 The first ferry line, between Brooklyn and Manhattan, is established.

1729 The first synagogue is built on Beaver Street.

1758 The first degrees are granted at Columbia University.

1761 The first street lights are lit.

1777 New York's first Governor, George Clinton, is elected.

1790 The first census of

New York City is taken.

1797 The first prison, Newgate, is opened .

1806 The first free school opens.

1827 The first black newspaper, Freedom's Journal, is founded

1869 The New York Times hires Maria Morgan, its first female reporter.

1916 The first zoning law is passed restricting building heights and zones.

1947 The subway fare is increased for the first

time from five to ten cents.

1989 The first black mayor of New York City, David Dinkins, is elected.

The most famous monument in New York City, the Statue of Liberty stands 151 feet high and has an eight-foot-long index finger! Unveiled in 1886 by President Grover Cleveland, a magnificent fireworks display celebrated her arrival, and the beginning of her long history as a symbol of America.

Introduction

When Irish immigrant Annie Moore arrived on Ellis Island in January 1892, she was greeted by a city of great contrasts. From its humble beginnings as a small colonial port in the 17th century, New York had developed into one of the most dynamic, prosperous and varied cities in the world. While the mansions of America's millionaires lined Fifth Avenue, thousands of European immigrants lived in crowded city tenements. On the occasion of consolidation in 1898, the five boroughs of Manhattan, Brooklyn, Queens, The Bronx and Staten Island were home to some of the richest and poorest families in America. At the same time, a distinctive multicultural society was developing, giving us a city that today has one of the most varied religious and ethnic mixes in the world. Modern New York is celebrated for many things, from its skyline, thriving cultural life of museums, concert halls, Broadway theaters, and galleries, to Wall Street and its unchallenged position as the world's economic epicenter. Even after the terrible events of September 11, 2001, in which thousands of New Yorkers lost their lives, the city stands proudly, remaining a symbol of the tolerance and open debate that characterize the modern world.

Dutch merchants first came to Manhattan Island to grow rich from trade in beaver fur. Hats and coats made from beaver fur were widely popular in 16th-century Europe, where people believed that wearing beaver fur ensured good health. Beaver Street in modern lower Manhattan honors the beaver's early importance.

Built in the late 19th century, the Dakota Apartments in Upper West Side is an exclusive New York address. Famous people such as Lauren Bacall, Judy Garland, and John Lennon have all lived here.

Verrazzano (1485–1528) was employed by France to find a faster route to Asia. He failed, but discovered Manhattan instead. Today the Verrazzano-Narrows Bridge links Staten Island to Brooklyn.

Henry Hudson

This British explorer sailed his ship the Half Moon (below) into Manhattan harbor in 1609. The Lenape greeted this amazing ship full of "swanekken," or "people of the salt water." Hudson (1565–1611) anchored and traded with the Lenape, then sailed up river. In modern New York, Hudson has a river, bridge, highway, park, and street named after him.

The Castello Plan

This map (below right) shows New Amsterdam in 1660. To the right is the 2,340-foot wall (now Wall Street) built in 1653 as protection against the British and Native Americans. The wide street at the top is was called Heerewegh or "the Long Highway," (now Broadway) along which colonists traveled to trade with the Lenape people outside the wall. Diamond-shaped Fort Amsterdam is at the island's tip. The canal in the center, later filled in by the British, is Broad Street.

8,000 BC – 1664

8,000 – 4,500 BC Lenape ancestors settle on Manhattan Island.

200 AD The Lenape start to farm corn.

1524 Giovanni da Verrazzano becomes the first European explorer to see Manhattan harbor.

Native Americans in the Manhattan area lived in longhouses built from curved branches and covered in bark and grass.

Dutch New Amsterdam

The Italian explorer Giovanni da Verrazzano sailed into New York harbor in 1524, describing it in his diary as merely "a pleasant place." Although he heard about the rich land cultivated by the Lenape people, whose ancestors had lived there for 6,000 years, he did not once leave his ship. In 1609, Henry Hudson entered the harbor and immediately recognized its great potential. He began a valuable fur trade with the Lenape on behalf of the Dutch West India Company, which quickly claimed the land and founded the colony of New Amsterdam in 1624. Two years later, the Dutch bought the whole island from the Lenape. In the beginning, New Amsterdam was a struggling, lawless community of just over 400 people. The arrival of Peter Stuyvesant in 1647 saw order established and stricter regulations imposed in the city.

New Amsterdam

In 1624 the Dutch West India Company sent 30 families to live in New Netherlands and establish the colony. While many settled inland, eight men stayed on Governors' Island. In 1625, six families joined them, and they moved to New Amsterdam at the southern tip of Manhattan. Within a year, they had cleared land and built bark cabins, Fort Amsterdam, a mill, a brewery, and a fur-trading post.

The first European settlement on Manhattan, 1624. The Lenape had named the land "Mana-hatta," or "hilly island."

1609 Henry Hudson anchors in the harbor and starts Dutch trade with the Lenape.

1624 The Dutch West India Company sends 110 people to the new colony of New Netherlands. Eight of them, soon joined by six families, establish a capital at New Amsterdam.

1625 The colonists build Fort Amsterdam. First Dutch child is born in New Amsterdam.

1626 More than 200 Europeans now live in New Amsterdam.

1643 Algonquian tribes, threatened by the new arrivals, burn colony villages and kill settlers.

1653 Stuyvesant grants the colonists limited self-government, and they build a 2,340-foot defensive wall.

1655 The Dutch West India Company allows Jews to settle in New Amsterdam.

1658 English sea captains petition their government against Dutch power in New Netherlands. New Amsterdam's first police force is established.

New Amsterdam is home to 1,500, including Dutch, English, French, Irish, German, Spanish, Polish, and Portuguese people. It is the most diverse colony in North America.

New York City's coat of arms displays two beavers, a windmill, and two barrels of flour – all symbols of New Amsterdam.

Peter Minuit buys Manhattan Island in 1626.

The Colonists Buy Manhattan

In 1626 Peter Minuit, Director-General of New Netherlands, met with Lenape leaders to negotiate the sale of Manhattan Island. He offered them Dutch goods (including axes, farming tools, and cloth) in exchange for the colonists' right to settle on Manhattan. The Lenape agreed, thinking that the "right to settle" was temporary, while the Dutch understood it to be permanent. The goods given to the tribes were worth 60 Dutch guilders, an amount equal to just over $500 today – less than the current price for a single monthly parking space in Manhattan!

The Dutch Influence

Typical Dutch constructions, such as windmills, canals, and narrow step-gabled houses, have all gone. There are reminders of the era, however, in lower Manhattan's street layout, and in Dutch names, such as Staten Island (Staaten Eylandt), the Bowery (the Bouwerie), and Brooklyn (Breuckelen). The remains of the gabled Stadt Huys (City Hall) are visible through a plexiglassed hole in the ground on Pearl Street.

The last Dutch house standing on Broad Street in the mid-19th century.

Peter Stuyvesant

Peter Stuyvesant (above), Director-General from 1647 to 1664, was renowned for his harshness and his pegleg. Before Stuyvesant, New Amsterdam was corrupt and slovenly: men gambled, drank, avoided church, and ignored laws. The Dutch West India Company told Stuyvesant to make the colony orderly and profitable, and to repair relations with the Lenape. Stuyvesant banned drinking on Sundays, outlawed knife-fighting in public, and imposed fines for missing church. Under his leadership the colonists founded a hospital, a school, a jail, and a post office. In 1653 he tried to expel Jews, but he was overruled. Today Manhattan's character owes a lot to its early emphasis on diversity and business.

1664 – 1783

August 27, 1664 The British capture New Amsterdam and rename it New York.

1673 The Dutch recapture the city, then trade it back to Britain a year later.

1682 Governor Thomas Dongan divides the New York area into counties: New York (Manhattan), Kings (Brooklyn), Richmond (Staten Island), and Queens.

1689 Dutch citizen Jacob Leisler's rebellion briefly seizes New York for William of Orange. Leisler is publicly executed in 1691.

1693 New York's first pavement is laid on Wall Street.

1695 The first paid fireman is appointed.

1703 4,375 people live in New York. Fewer than half are Dutch.

1711 A slave market opens by the East River.

1725 The first local newspaper, the New York Gazette, is published.

1741 32 slaves are killed for rebellious acts.

1765 New York merchants start to boycott English goods until the oppressive Stamp Act tax is repealed.

1776 The British drive the Colonial Army from New York and station

British New York

Federal-style townhouses have front doors with classical columns and fanlights, such as 59 Morton Street today.

New York in 1767

The New York of 1767 (above), surveyed by Bernard Ratzer, shows densely-populated streets extending north to today's City Hall Park, and wharves lining the East River. Farther north lay farms owned by rich landowners like James de Lancey, and country estates such as the Morris-Jumel Mansion, which still stands in Harlem. Some of the names remaining today from British times include Queens, Hanover Square and Greenwich Village.

Dutch rule of New Amsterdam lasted only 40 years. The British coveted their Dutch enemy's colony, which became increasingly vulnerable over the years until 1664, when the Dutch surrendered to British troops without a fight. Renamed New York, after the Duke of York, who had been promised the colony as a present from his brother King Charles II, the British slowly imposed their own laws, trading rules, and government. The British ruled a bustling, lively city for 119 years, until increasing taxes and general discontent saw the beginnings of the Revolutionary War. When the Revolutionaries won in 1783, the British retreated and New York became the new nation's capital.

Above: Map of New York in 1767, by British army officer Bernard Ratzer.

Peter Stuyvesant surrenders the Dutch colony to the British.

The Dutch Surrender

On August 27, 1664, four British warships anchored in the harbor. Peter Stuyvesant prepared for battle from Fort Amsterdam, saying, "I would rather be carried to my grave than surrender." The Dutch colonists preferred to give in, however, and petitioned him to avoid "absolute ruin and destruction." With only a small army of soldiers and

In colonial times, citizens encouraged pigs to wander the streets, eating the garbage to keep them clean. Most of New York's streets remained unpaved until the late 1700s.

A British Colony

In lively British New York, people met in streets, coffeehouses, and more than 150 taverns, where they received mail, bartered, and gossiped. Merchants lived over their shops. Colonists built the city's first synagogue in

listless citizens behind him, Stuyvesant surrendered nine days later, without firing a single shot.

1729 and many churches were built at this time too, including St. Paul's Chapel (1766), now the oldest church in New York. They erected the first public theater in 1732, and lit the first gas street lights in 1761. Dutch traditions continued alongside British customs for many years.

10,000 there. A fire destroys one-third of the city.

1783 The British retreat and Washington marches into New York, now an American city of roughly 12,000 people.

Most slaves were sold at slave markets like this one.

The Slave Market

The British abolished Dutch rules that allowed slaves to marry, own land, and buy partial freedom in old age. They built a slave market in 1711 on the East River end of Wall Street. By the 1720s, one in every five households owned slaves, most of whom worked as domestic servants. New York's 2,000 slaves resisted daily. In 1712, the first slave revolt occurred when slaves set fire to the home of a wealthy New Yorker, then killed the men who came to extinguish it. Accusations of a slave plot in 1741 led to a trial of all black New Yorkers and the torturous killing of 32. Slavery was finally outlawed in 1827.

A Revolutionary soldier.

Below: South side of John Street, between William and Nassau Streets, 1768.

Southeast view of New York Harbor in 1765.

George Washington re-enters New York in 1783.

The Great Port

By 1740, New York was the third largest port in the British Empire, after London and Philadelphia. Britain fought with France in 1756, and stationed 39,000 soldiers in New York, from where they could sail to attack French colonies. New York's merchants were very happy, as money flowed into their shops for the next seven years.

The Revolutionary War

British warships arrived in New York in 1776. George Washington and the Colonial Army retreated, and the British seized New York. They controlled it from 1776 until 1783, making it the only American city occupied for most of the Revolutionary War. When the war ended on November 25, 1783, Washington re-entered the city and gave his farewell address to the troops at the Fraunces Tavern. The British troops and Loyalists left, and Patriots returned to celebrate. They destroyed most signs of British life in the city.

The Stamp Act

The Stamp Act of 1765, yet another tax imposed by the British on the colonies, added to mounting American anger over British rule. New Yorkers were strongly opposed to the new tax and the city hosted the Stamp Act Congress during which delegates from the

An example of the hated stamps which were to be affixed to all documents, newspapers, and even playing cards.

13 colonies proclaimed the tax illegitimate. The Sons of Liberty was also formed with the aim of ousting the British from American shores. The stage was set for the American Revolution.

A Revolutionary nails the Stars and Stripes, with 13 stars representing the original 13 states of the Federation, to a flagpole in New York Harbor.

George Washington's inauguration as first president of the United States at Federal Hall.

Federal Hall

When New York became the official capital in 1788, its City Hall was transformed into lavish Federal Hall. George Washington was inaugurated there as the first United States president on April 30, 1789. In 1790, however, Secretary of the Treasury, Alexander Hamilton, traded New York's capital status in exchange for the federal repayment of its war debt, and the capital moved to Philadelphia. Federal Hall became City Hall once again, until a new one was built in 1812. Federal Hall National Memorial (built in 1842) still stands on its original site on Wall Street.

Federal Hall in 1797.

1783 – 1825

This statue of George Washington stands today at Federal Hall National Memorial, on the spot where he was inaugurated.

Reinventing the City

After the Revolutionary War, New York quickly discarded all remaining signs of British rule, rebuilding the ruined city, renaming streets, and entering into an energetic period of rapid growth. By 1800 its population had almost doubled, and the foundations were being laid for its transformation into a rich and powerful city. Banks and offices began to appear along Wall Street, Broadway was lined with elegant shops, while coffeehouses, taverns, and theaters sprang up throughout the city. By 1811, New York had expanded so far north that a grid plan for Manhattan's future streets was created.

The Tontine Coffee House in 1796.

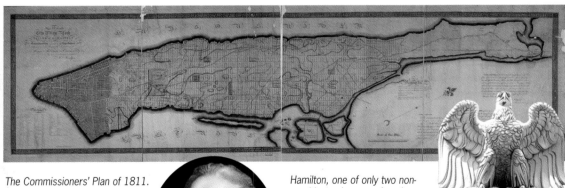

The Commissioners' Plan of 1811.

Commissioners' Plan of 1811

Mayor of New York from 1803 to 1815, DeWitt Clinton worried about New York's rapid expansion and established a commission to decide how Manhattan Island should develop. The plan (above) was a grid of streets and avenues cut in rectangular lots, with Broadway at an angle. With the notable exception of Central Park, New York City follows that plan today.

Alexander Hamilton

Born in 1755 into an obscure family in the West Indies, Hamilton studied at King's College (later Columbia University) in New York in 1773. He believed that New York's enterprise, creativity, immigrant population, and flair for commerce pointed to America's future. In 1784 he founded the Bank of New York and became the first Secretary of the Treasury, under President George Washington. Hamilton's visionary policies led to the creation of the New York Stock Exchange in 1792, helping to secure the city's future wealth and power.

Hamilton, one of only two non-presidents shown on American bank notes, appears on the $10 bill.

After the Revolution, New Yorkers replaced the royal crown on their coat of arms with an eagle, a symbol of liberty during the war.

In 1804, Hamilton was killed in a duel with rival New Yorker Aaron Burr.

1783 New York's population of 12,000 doubles over the next three years.

1784 Alexander Hamilton founds the Bank of New York.

1788 New York becomes the capital of the new nation.

1790 The first census puts New York's population at 33,000.

1792 The first stock market opens on Wall Street. It moves to Tontine Coffee House a year later.

1793 New York's buildings are given numbered addresses.

1794 The Jay Treaty, negotiated by Chief Justice John Jay, maintains peace with Britain.

1797 New Yorkers replace British currency with dollars, dimes, and cents.

1798 Yellow fever kills 2,086.

1804 New York, with

80,000 citizens, is the largest city in America.

1811 The Commissioners' Plan designs the city's future grid layout.

1812 America declares war on Britain, whose ships blockade New York Harbor. The war ends in 1814.

1814 The steamship "Fulton the First" embarks from New York Harbor.

1817–1825 9,000 men build the Erie Canal.

1820 New York becomes the nation's largest city.

Fulton the First

Crowds cheered when steamship pioneer Robert Fulton launched his steam frigate "Fulton the First" from New York Harbor in 1814. New York's East River waterfront was known as the "Street of Ships," one of the world's greatest centers of shipping and commerce. New Yorkers started the first scheduled trans-Atlantic shipping service in 1818, inventing the idea (and the term) of arriving "on time."

1814 launch of steam frigate "Fulton the First" from New York Harbor.

The New York Stock Exchange

Hamilton's finance program, launched in 1791, and the "Buttonwood Agreement" between brokers a year later, established the first stock exchange on Wall Street. It soon moved to the Tontine Coffee House on the corner of Wall and Water Streets, where brokers and merchants traded shares and auctioned barrels of cotton, rice, sugar, tea, rum, and other goods. Brokers stood on the curb at Broad Street, gesturing to colleagues in the Tontine's windows, a system that became the New York Curb Exchange, then the American Stock Exchange. Now, on average, more than $170 million passes through the New York Stock Exchange every trading day.

Along Wall Street (above), Alexander Hamilton lived at number 57, his Bank of New York was at 56, his Bank of the United States at 52, and the Continental Congress's temporary headquarters at number 40.

Early Dutch immigrants ate "koekjes," but New Yorkers first made cookies widely popular in the 1800s. German and Dutch immigrants called these cookies (above) "Shnecken Noodles," "Schneckenoodles," or "Snickerdoodles."

A fashionable New York lady dressed for a ball in about 1824.

Entertainment

Fashionable New Yorkers attended the Park Theater, opened in 1798 on elegant Park Row, which could seat 2,400. Other amusements included Dr. King's exhibition of orangutans and porcupines on Wall Street, Pepe and Beschard's Circus on Broadway, and the taverns, which offered gambling (made illegal in 1788), dog-fighting, musical concerts, and puppet shows. Many people had gaming tables at home, where they played backgammon and chess in the evenings.

The Park Theater in 1822.

John Jacob Astor

The richest man in America at the time of his death, John Jacob Astor (left) traded furs and used his profits to buy undeveloped Manhattan land. He waited for New Yorkers to move northward, then resold the land at the most expensive prices in the world. He resold most of the Lower East Side and all of the land under today's Times Square. He was known for both his enormous wealth and poor table manners, which included using a knife to eat peas with ice cream!

THE BROOKLYN BRIDGE

1814 The first regular steam ferry service connects Brooklyn to Manhattan.

1869 Work begins on the Brooklyn Bridge. Roebling dies and his son,

Washington Roebling, becomes the new engineer.

1871 Bridge workers strike, but stop when threatened with losing their jobs.

1873 Washington Roebling is afflicted with "the bends". Over the next decade he watches the

bridge's construction through a telescope from his window, relying on letters and his wife, Emily, to convey his directions

1876 The bridge's two towers are finished.

1877 Demolition of buildings on the New York side begins. A temporary

footpath is erected between the two towers.

1880 Brooklyn, home to 600,000, is the third-largest city in America.

1883 The Brooklyn Bridge opens. 150,000 people pay the one cent toll to walk across.

The Roeblings

John Augustus Roebling emigrated from Germany in 1831. He built iron bridges for the railways before becoming chief engineer of the Brooklyn Bridge in 1867. He lived just long enough to complete its designs in 1869. His son Washington Roebling oversaw construction of the bridge, but not without difficulty. After 1873, illness forced Roebling Jr. to work from home, supervising the job through a telescope from Columbia Heights, Brooklyn. Too sick to attend the opening celebration, he

1884 P.T. Barnum leads 21 elephants across the Brooklyn Bridge walkway, then declares it safe.

1886 Steve Brodie claims to have survived a jump off the Brooklyn Bridge.

sent the message: "Why not just put up a sign saying, 'The Bridge is Open'?"

Manhattan has 17 bridges, and New York City nearly 770, but it is the Brooklyn Bridge, opened in 1883, which is described as "the Great Bridge." Spanning the East River between Manhattan and Brooklyn, it has inspired many artists, writers, and filmmakers, and encouraged engineers and designers to rethink their professional roles. A marvel of world engineering, providing a magnificent gateway to the city, the Brooklyn Bridge expressed the spirit of the age: ambition, progress, and size.

The Brooklyn Bridge

The Brooklyn Bridge needed to be high enough to avoid the dangerous waters of the East River at high tide, and the tallest sailing ships. Roebling's solution was to build what was then the world's largest suspension bridge. It is supported by four steel cables strung over two towers rising 276 feet above the water. Two seven-story stone anchorages hold the cables firm on the Brooklyn and Manhattan shores. The bridge measures 5,989 feet, 1,595 of which span the river.

More than 5,000 men built the bridge, working in three eight-hour shifts every day but Sunday. Most were immigrant laborers. They finished the Brooklyn tower in 1875, and the New York tower in 1876.

Several people aimed to survive a jump off the Brooklyn Bridge shortly after it opened. Swimming instructor Robert E. Odlum (left) jumped on May 19, 1885, but died almost instantly from internal bleeding. A year later, Steve Brodie claimed to have survived the jump, though no one witnessed this feat.

Crowds gathered to watch as Master Mechanic E.F. Farrington then hauled himself across the incomplete bridge on a tiny seat attached to wire rope.

The Opening Ceremony

The Brooklyn Bridge opened in May 1883 with a spectacular, day-long celebration. 150,000 New Yorkers walked across the bridge and marvelled at the views of the river and the Manhattan skyline. That evening the city put on its greatest fireworks display ever: 10,000 pieces, followed by 500 rockets fired simultaneously.

Tragically, a week after the opening ceremony, a panic on the bridge killed 12 people. A woman crossing the bridge lost her footing, fell down a staircase, and screamed. People thought the bridge was collapsing and stampeded.

In 1884, the showman P.T. Barnum transported 21 elephants, including a six-and-a-half-ton jumbo, across the bridge. After they reached the other side, Barnum declared the bridge safe and won himself – and his circus elephants – great publicity.

1890 Brooklyn's population approaches 800,000.

1898 Brooklyn becomes part of Greater New York.

1924 Regular steam ferry service between Brooklyn and Manhattan stops.

John Augustus Roebling (left) and his son, Washington Roebling (right).

When the bridge opened, 250,000 people used it every day to get to work. Thousands traveled on the Manhattan transit cars and the Brooklyn trolleys that ran on either side of the central pedestrian walkway. Others rode across in horse-drawn vehicles in the two outer lanes. Fewer and fewer people used the Brooklyn-to-Manhattan ferries, which stopped running in 1924.

The Brooklyn Bridge soon after it was opened.

SAFE FOR ONLY 25 MEN AT ONE TIME DO NOT WALK CLOSE TOGETHER NOR RUN, JUMP OR TROT. BREAK STEP! W.A. Roebling *Eng in Chief*

Horse-Drawn Vehicles

For years, horses provided most of the transportation in New York City. They pulled carriages, omnibuses, street cars, railcars, fire engines, and ambulances. In 1882, electricity became available in the city. By 1887 electric street cars were starting to replace horse-drawn vehicles.

Traffic in 19th-century New York moved slowly with horse-drawn vehicles like the horse railway.

The "El"

When New York's streets became overcrowded in the mid-1800s, city leaders suggested an elevated railway line, and in 1868 the city's first "el" started along Greenwich Street. Soon "els" ran on Second, Third, Sixth, and Ninth Avenues, and linked Manhattan to Brooklyn and the Bronx. They were suspended in 1955.

The New York Path-Finder, published in 1848, listed details of the bewildering number of ferries, railroads, omnibuses, stage-coaches, and express trains that operated in and around the city.

Bowery and Doubledeck Elevated Rail Road (right).

Buses

The first regular public transportation was the horse-drawn omnibus (stagecoach) that ran along Broadway in the early 1830s. Coaches like the Fifth Avenue Bus (right), could carry roughly 20 passengers, and complete a round trip along Fifth Avenue in an hour and a half. Modern New York has around 4,000 motorized buses that run along 200 routes and 1,000 miles of streets. Today passengers can get free transfers between New York City's buses and its subways.

Many New Yorkers don't know how to drive a car. With the public transportation available in the city, they've never needed to. Besides, parking prices are astronomically high. Those who do drive in Manhattan travel along one-way streets: even-numbered streets run east, and odd-numbered streets run west.

TRANSPORTATION

1638 The first ferry line runs between Manhattan and Brooklyn.

1693 The Kingsbridge connects Manhattan Island to the mainland.

1713 The Staten Island Ferry begins operation.

Moving Around Town

The sheer size of New York has caused a unique transportation system to develop over the years. Its famous yellow taxi cabs are sometimes the only vehicles to be seen on Manhattan streets, while its massive subway system enables millions of New Yorkers to travel around the city every day. Initially travel between Manhattan and the neighborhoods of Brooklyn, Queens, the Bronx and Staten Island took place by boat. As the city grew, the boroughs were linked by bridges and public ferries. On the streets of the city itself, people moved around in horse-drawn carriages, omnibuses, and street cars until, in the mid 1800s, an ever increasing population called for a better means of transportation. The city's first elevated railway operated for almost 100 years until it gradually was replaced by the subway.

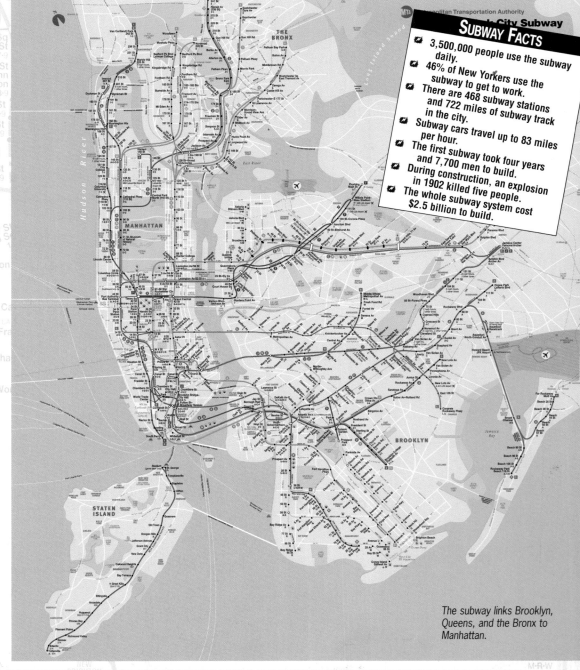

SUBWAY FACTS

- 3,500,000 people use the subway daily.
- 46% of New Yorkers use the subway to get to work.
- There are 468 subway stations and 722 miles of subway track in the city.
- Subway cars travel up to 83 miles per hour.
- The first subway took four years and 7,700 men to build.
- During construction, an explosion in 1902 killed five people.
- The whole subway system cost $2.5 billion to build.

The subway links Brooklyn, Queens, and the Bronx to Manhattan.

The Subway

In 1900, work started on an electrically-powered subway that would cross the city to the outer boroughs. The first subway opened in 1904 and, despite what skeptics had predicted about "holes in the ground," New Yorkers loved it. Within four years, nearly a million people rode the subway each day.

1832 The city's (and the world's) first street railway, the horse-drawn New York and Harlem Railroad, starts operation.

1868 The Brooklyn ferries carry 48,000,000 passengers this year.

1870 The Beach Pneumatic

Railway opens under Broadway carrying 400,000 passengers in its first year.

1871 Grand Central Depot opens on 42nd Street.

1883 The Brooklyn Bridge opens.

1887 Electric street cars start operation.

1900 Construction begins on the subway used today.

1904 New York's first subway opens, running from City Hall to 145th Street. The ride costs five cents, and takes 26 minutes.

1907 The first metered taxi cabs begin operation

1913 Today's Grand Central Terminal opens.

1917 The last horse-drawn car stops operation.

1927 The Holland Tunnel, the world's first underwater vehicular roadway, opens.

1946 The subway system carries a record

8,872,244 passengers on December 23.

1955 The Transit Authority is created to oversee the subway and bus systems.

1957 Street cars, made obsolete by the subway, cease to run.

Grand Central Terminal

Roughly 140,000 commuters pass through Grand Central Terminal on 42nd Street each day. This striking building, which stretches for three blocks, was completed in 1913 on the site of Grand Central Depot. The vast Main Concourse area was inspired by ancient Roman bathhouses, and features constellations on the ceiling. Grand Central Station is at the heart of New York's subway system and its commuter railway lines.

The beautiful clock on Grand Central's south facade, is topped by Mercury, the ancient Roman god of speed.

Airports

New York City is served by three airports. La Guardia, in Queens, was built in 1939 under the direction of Fiorello La Guardia, New York's highly respected mayor. When it opened, Mayor La Guardia wrote to President Roosevelt, "It's the greatest, the best, the most up-to-date airport in the U.S." John F. Kennedy International Airport ("JFK") in Queens is now one of the world's busiest airports. Newark International Airport is in New Jersey, but only 16 miles from Manhattan. In 2000, these three airports handled a total of 92,200,000 passengers.

Plane preparing for take-off at Newark Airport, New Jersey.

Taxi!

The yellow taxi cab (below) is a favorite symbol of New York City. Taxis, which dart through busy traffic at high speed, can take people anywhere in the city. There are few taxi

Taxi cab in Times Square.

stands, but New Yorkers have perfected the art of hailing taxis as they whiz past in the streets. The first metered taxis appeared on New York's streets in 1907, just after cars were invented.

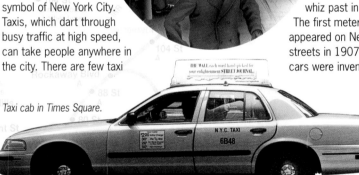

TAXI FACTS

- There are 11,800 licensed yellow taxis in New York City.
- Taxis are licensed by the New York City Taxi and Limousine Commission.
- This Commission has installed audio messages, read by celebrities such as Judd Hirsch (of the TV show "Taxi") and opera singer Placido Domingo, to remind passengers to use seat belts and remember their belongings.
- In May 2000, the cellist Lynn Harrell left his $4 million Stradivarius cello behind in a taxi. The driver, Mohamed Ibrahim, returned it to him the next day. Yo-Yo Ma left his $2.5 million instrument in a taxi in 1999, and also recovered it unharmed.
- The last old-fashioned Checker taxi cab was retired in July 1999.
- The Website www.taxicam.com gives live video coverage of New York City from the hood of an operating taxi.
- There are 35,000 "gypsy," or unlicensed, taxis in New York City.

Ferries

The first New York ferry ran between Brooklyn and Manhattan in 1638. For centuries, transportation by water was the only way to travel from the outer boroughs of Staten Island, Queens, and Brooklyn to the island of Manhattan. The first Staten Island Ferry started operation in 1713, and in 1905 the Municipal Staten Island Ferry opened with a five cent fare. Today the ride is free, and offers the best views of the Statue of Liberty.

Helicopters

Traveling by helicopter in New York is an exciting change from ground-based travel. Helicopters can be seen regularly flying over the city. Even tour companies offer scenic rides above the city, with spectacular views of Manhattan's skyline.

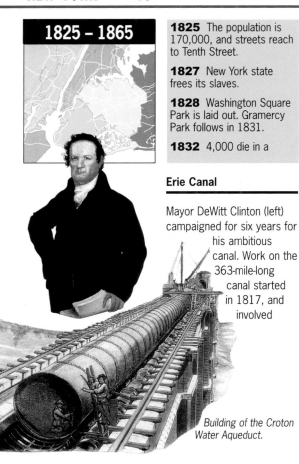

1825 – 1865

1825 The population is 170,000, and streets reach to Tenth Street.

1827 New York state frees its slaves.

1828 Washington Square Park is laid out. Gramercy Park follows in 1831.

1832 4,000 die in a cholera epidemic.

1841 P.T. Barnum opens his American Museum of Curiosities on Broadway.

1846 The first baseball game is played in New York.

1849 Anti-British rioters attack the Astor Place Opera House, where British actor William Macready is performing in Macbeth.

1851 The New York Daily Times (today's New York Times) begins publication.

1853 World's Fair opens.

1854 Academy of Music opens.

1855 Manhattan's Castle Garden becomes America's first immigrant processing center. In this period, at least 320,000 immigrants

Erie Canal

Mayor DeWitt Clinton (left) campaigned for six years for his ambitious canal. Work on the 363-mile-long canal started in 1817, and involved 9,000 men, each working for less than $1 a day. Officially opened in October 1825, shipping a ton of wheat from Buffalo to New York now took eight days (not three weeks) and cost $6 (not $100). New York rapidly became the center of American commerce.

Building of the Croton Water Aqueduct.

The Great Fire of 1835

In December 1835, a fire destroyed 674 buildings in the city's densely-packed business district, including warehouses, offices, banks, and all traces of New Amsterdam. Within a year, all the burned lots were resold at inflated prices, and the area was rebuilt.

After the Great Fire of 1835, 23 of New York's 25 fire insurance companies were forced into bankruptcy.

The Metropolis

Croton Water Works

A modern system of tunnels, aqueducts, and reservoirs, the Croton Water Works opened in 1842, supplying New Yorkers with clean water from upstate, and making indoor plumbing possible. The Croton Water Reservoir stood on the site of today's New York Public Library.

Merchants on Wall Street at half-past two on October 13, 1857, the worst day of the panic of 1857. By three o'clock 18 banks had suspended payments.

Wall Street Panic of 1857

In 1857 a mixture of corruption and bad luck triggered an economic crises on Wall Street. About 25,000 workers lost their jobs, 100,000 more lost their homes, and many rich New Yorkers went bankrupt.

Five Points

The notorious Five Points slum (below) spread outward from today's Foley Square. Greedy landlords packed immigrants and former slaves into old buildings, which stood on sinking, reeking land. Drunks, prostitutes, and gangs roamed the streets. The most crowded place in 1850s America, it was a breeding-ground for deadly yellow fever. Uptown, the richer classes worried about the morals of the slum residents, and sent social workers to reform them. (See Immigration, pages 22–23.)

I n 1825, New York was an orderly, peaceful city with a population of less than 170,000. The majority of New Yorkers were native-born and lived a simple, almost rural life. By 1865, however, population figures had soared, and the city had changed dramatically. Over the next 40 years, roads were paved and widened, a water system was laid, many large buildings were built, and Central Park was created. Walt Whitman wrote of New York's "rabid feverish itching for change" as it quickly developed into the biggest metropolis in America, becoming a city of stark contrasts. Defined by its extremes of social, economic and moral values, late 19th century New York was a city of elegant balls, popular music halls, poverty, and crime, wrestling with the particular problems and complexities of modern, urban life.

arrive ech year.

1858 Baseball fans are charged an admission fee for the first time.

1859 Cooper Union, a center for debate and free education, is founded.

1860 Central Park is completed. Population

reaches 813,669.

1861 The Civil War begins and 250,000 New Yorkers rally in Union Square.

1863 50,000 immigrants riot against the Civil War draft in Manhattan.

1865 The Unionists win the Civil War.

Ice skating in Central Park was so popular in 1862 that Vanity Fair magazine published "Hints to Skaters."

Central Park

Central Park opened in 1860. Its co-designer Frederick Law Olmsted wanted it to give peace, beauty, and a sense of urban community to rich and poor New Yorkers alike. "The park should be an antithesis to [the city's] bustling, paved, rectangular, walled-in streets," he wrote. Until 1934 the Sheep's Meadow held a flock of sheep, and the Dairy a herd of cows. Today Central Park blends Olmsted and Calvert Vaux's vision of serene, rural vistas with modern interests like baseball, bicycling, running, and roller-blading.

Fashionable New Yorkers paraded in horse-drawn carriages through the park.

# of America

These New Yorkers are dressed for an afternoon walk. The woman is wearing a walking ensemble from one of the elegant stores along Broadway or Fifth Avenue.

The Civil War Ends

Supported by the industrial strength of New York and other northern cities, the Unionists won the war. On April 3, 1865, telegraph offices on Wall Street reported the news, and New Yorkers poured into the streets to celebrate. Only two weeks later they gathered again to mourn the death of Abraham Lincoln (above). His 1865 funeral train passed through New York, and hundreds of thousands of people stood along Broadway, watching in silence.

Printing House Square

Dozens of newspapers reported from Park Row, close to both City Hall and the notorious Five

Points slum. "Printing House Square" (above) on Park Row was the location of the Sun, Tribune, Herald, Post, and Times buildings.

Civil War Riots

When the Civil War began, New York was the heart of the industrial, Unionist North. Poor immigrants were drafted to fight, while rich men bought their way out for $300. Angry Irish immigrants blamed African-Americans for

the war and rioted in 1863. They burned and looted shops, houses, the draft office, the Colored Orphan Asylum, and they lynched 11 men. Union troops stopped the violence (above), but thousands of African-Americans fled the city.

Walt Whitman

Born on Long Island in 1819, the poet Walt Whitman (right) spent most of his life in Manhattan. He worked as a

journalist, but also wandered the streets, writing of the "fascinating chaos," the "modernity", and the "bustle, the show, the glitter, and even the gaudiness" of the

metropolis. He wrote the poem "O Captain! My Captain!" about Abraham Lincoln's death.

ARCHITECTURE

1857 Elisha Otis installs the first passenger elevator in the Haughwout Building on Broadway.

1869 America's first apartment house, The Stuyvesant, is built on East 18th Street.

1884 The Dakota Apartments open near Central Park West.

1888 A steel building skeleton is first used to construct the Tower Building on Broadway.

1913 The Woolworth Building is the world's tallest building at 792 feet.

1916 America's first zoning law is passed, which restricts the width and height of buildings and divides New York into commercial and residential zones.

1930 The Chrysler Building is the world's tallest building at 1,048 feet.

1931 The Empire State

Building is the world's tallest building at 1,250 feet.

1932 In the movie "King Kong," a giant ape scales the Empire State Building.

1947 The UNs' Secretariat building is the city's first "glass box" building.

1965 The Landmarks Preservation Commission is

formed to save the city's architectural heritage.

1975 The Twin Towers of the World Trade Center are the world's tallest buildings at 1,350 feet.

1993 The 52-story Four Seasons Hotel becomes the city's tallest hotel.

2001 Commercial airliners

hijacked by Arab terrorists bring down the Twin Towers.

Below: The Empire State Building's mast tower is colorfully lit for occasions throughout the year: green on St. Patrick's Day, red, white, and blue on Independence Day, orange on Halloween, and red and green at Christmas.

N ew York's towering skyscrapers were designed not just for limited space, but also to advertise the power, success, and prestige of their owners. By 1902, the downtown skyline already existed, with 66 skyscrapers clustered around Wall Street. In the 1930s, more skyscrapers were built in Manhattan's business district, which led to the development of the striking midtown skyline. Today the Art Deco style Chrysler Building along with the world famous Empire State Building and the "glass box" skyscrapers of the 1960s serve to express New York's unique architectural heritage.

The Skyline

Art Deco

A 1925 Paris exposition of Modern Industrial and Decorative Arts introduced the style of building decoration that was embraced by New Yorkers as Art Deco, a style that used a range of forms inspired by ancient Egypt, Mayan culture, modern technology, and other sources, reproducing them using modern materials like glass, steel, and chrome.

Manhattan has two main skylines. The midtown skyline is visible across the center of Manhattan, and the downtown skyline is visible at the tip of the island.

The blue-green colors of the former McGraw-Hill Building at 330 W. 42nd Street are a fine example of New York's Art Deco.

"Glass Box" Skyscrapers

New York's first "glass box" was the 1947 United Nations' Secretariat Building, a 544-foot-tall slab with white marble end walls and green glass side walls, set in an aluminium grid. Today dozens of corporate headquarters are located in "glass boxes."

This magnificent wall decoration is from the lobby of the Empire State Building.

The Empire State Building

The magnificent Empire State Building, designed by the architects Shreve, Lamb, and Harmon, has been regarded as the quintessential skyscraper and a romantic symbol of New York City since its opening in 1931. Completing this 102-story

The Chrysler Building

The automobile magnate Walter P. Chrysler commissioned the Chrysler Building (right) to express the luxury of the Jazz Age

structure at the height of the Great Depression (see page 28) was an act of tremendous faith in the city's future. The Empire State Building remained half-empty until the 1940s, but tourists immediately flocked to its 86th and 102nd floor observation decks for spectacular views over Manhattan.

and the industrial precision of his cars. The Chrysler Building is a prime example of Art Deco style.

Right: The Chrysler Building

EMPIRE STATE BUILDING FACTS

- Cost: $40,498,000
- Building height: 1,250 feet
- Height to tower tip: 1,472 feet
- Weight: 365,000 tons
- Bricks: 10,000,000
- Stories: 102
- Windows: 6,500
- Elevators: 62

Men at Work

More than 3,400 men built the Empire State Building, constructing four and a half steel-framed stories each week. Jobs were scarce, and workers risked their lives daily, laboring on narrow platforms and steel girders at dizzying heights. The photographer Lewis W. Hine scaled the unfinished building with them to record their labor and achievements. He published his world-famous images of these heroic men defying gravity in the book *Men at Work*.

"The 400"

Mrs. William B. Astor kept an influential list of the most socially desirable New Yorkers. She restricted it to 400 people, the number that could fit into the ballroom in her Fifth Avenue mansion.

Astor House ballroom during a ball.

1865 – 1898

1865 The Citizens' Association of New York conducts the nation's first sanitary survey. 900,000 people live in the city.

1866 The Atlantic telegraph cable links New York directly to London.

1873 Tammany Hall boss William Tweed is convicted of fraud. Panic on Wall Street sparks the first depression.

1878 New York's first telephone directory, a double-sided card with 252 names, is published. Today's Yellow Pages alone has 1,558 pages of listings.

1888 New Yorkers hold the first "ticker tape parade." Over 200 people die in the Great Blizzard.

1891 Carnegie Hall opens

New York's lavish social events were reported across the country. At the Vanderbilt ball in May 1883, Alice Vanderbilt, inspired by the introduction of such lighting to lower Manhattan six months earlier, came dressed as "Electric Light" (left).

Fifth Avenue

Fifth Avenue with the Vanderbilt mansion in 1883.

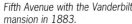

By 1892, almost half of America's millionaires (1,800) lived in New York, including Cornelius Vanderbilt, Andrew Carnegie, J.P. Morgan, and John D. Rockefeller. They built lavish mansions that stretched for two miles along upper Fifth Avenue. In later years exclusive shops replaced many of these buildings, but a few remain today, including the Metropolitan Club or "Millionaires' Club" and the Cooper-Hewitt Museum (finished in 1901).

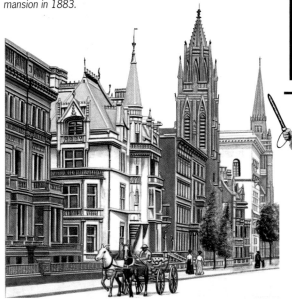

Bright Lights,

Boss Tweed

Boss William M. Tweed, leader of the political organization Tammany Hall, was the most corrupt city politician in American history. He stole more than $6 million from city taxes. Thomas Nast's Harper's Weekly cartoons (shown

here, left and right) helped to expose the graft.

I n 1865 New York emerged from four years of Civil War as the second largest financial center in the world. In the following years, railroads linked it to the American west, the Atlantic cable connected it to London, and Thomas Edison made it the first electrically-lit city in the world. Some of the wealthiest men in the country built their mansions on Fifth Avenue, and the first skyscrapers and department stores expressed the city's forward-looking urban spirit. The city, however, also was home to almost a million poverty-stricken immigrants, the ranks of whom swelled every day with new arrivals.

"How the Other Half Lives"

In 1890, Jacob A. Riis published his book *How the Other Half Lives*, a collection of photographs and text that captured the wretched living conditions in New York's slums. By that time roughly 1,000,000 immigrants lived in 40,000 tenement houses in lower Manhattan. Lacking sufficient clothing and adequate food, they lived packed together into rooms without fresh air, light, or plumbing. Riis's book shocked and educated the public, and activists tried to improve the sanitation, health conditions, and population density of the tenements. Old tenement buildings still stand on Manhattan's Eldridge Street.
(See also Immigration, pages 22–23.)

Right: Baxter Street Court slums in 1890.

Left: Italian ragpicker and child at home in 1889.

with a five-day music festival, featuring Tchaikovsky conducting his own works.

1892 Ellis Island opens as an immigration processing center. New York's population is two million.

1898 The city incorporates the outer boroughs of Brooklyn, Bronx, Queens, and Staten Island, becoming Greater New York with a population of 3.5 million.

The Beach Pneumatic Railway (right) began operating in 1870.

Commodore of the Railroads

Cornelius Vanderbilt grew rich through the shipping industry (where they called him "the Commodore"), then invested his money in railroads. He united a number of

small railway lines into the New York Central Railroad, and in 1871 he built Grand Central Depot on 42nd Street. Virtually all trains from the Mississippi River to New England passed through Grand Central, making Vanderbilt the richest man in America.

Left: A cartoon showing Cornelius Vanderbilt controlling the Hudson River and New York Central Railways.

City Transport

As more people arrived, they spread uptown and to the boroughs, crowding the streets with horses, carriages, and omnibuses. The city desperately needed new forms of public transportation. Solutions of this era included the Metropolitan Elevated Railway ("el"), running above ground, and the city's first subway, the Beach Pneumatic Railway, running beneath it.

The Statue of Liberty

The most famous symbol of American freedom was a gift from the French Republic. Sculpted by Frédéric-Auguste Bartholdi and engineered by Gustave Eiffel, "Liberty Enlightening the World" arrived in New York in 1884, carefully packed in pieces into boxes. Its right hand and torch had been on display in Madison Square for years, to help raise funds for a pedestal. Thousands of people donated money, and in 1886 the pedestal and statue were erected with fanfare. Today the Statue of Liberty stands on Liberty Island to greet new arrivals to the city.

138 feet high, the Statue of Liberty is one of the most famous landmarks in New York.

Big City

Thomas Edison, shown here with his light bulb, also invented the phonograph for recording sound. He wanted to install a phonograph in the Statue of Liberty so she could whistle at boats, but New York turned him down.

Early skyscrapers

At the start of this era, five storey buildings lined the streets, with only a few commercial structures reaching the amazing height of eight storeys. Cast-iron construction, introduced to New York in 1848, could support many more storeys, but no one wanted to walk up that many stairs. Then in 1857, Elisha Graves Otis installed the

The Flatiron Building today.

world's first passenger elevator in the cast-iron Haughwout Building, which still stands on Broome Street and Broadway. In the late 1880s, steel-frame construction and electrically-run elevators would lead to buildings of unprecedented height. The 22-story Flatiron Building built in 1902 (left) stands at the intersection of Broadway and Fifth Avenue.

Bright Lights

At first New York was lit at night by flickering gaslights. In the 1880s, the city experimented with expensive arc lights. These burned out quickly and emitted noxious fumes, but they thrilled New Yorkers on

Broadway in 1881 (above left). In 1882, Thomas Edison created incandescent electric lighting, which he installed along 50 blocks in the financial district. Soon houses, department stores, theaters, and restaurants installed his invention.

Greater New York

While New York had grown into America's largest city, the city of Brooklyn had become its third largest (with 650,000 inhabitants), and the semi-rural provinces of Queens, Staten Island, and the Bronx were home to 150,000, 67,000 and 200,000 people respectively. In 1898 New York's government consolidated Manhattan, Brooklyn, Queens, Staten Island, and the Bronx (now called the five boroughs) into one city of 3,360,000 people covering 359 square miles. Only London had more people and power than New York City. Ferries, trains, and bridges carried people to all corners of the vast city.

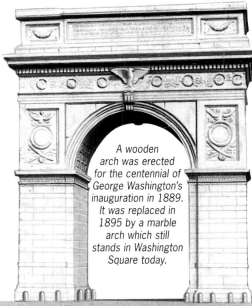

A wooden arch was erected for the centennial of George Washington's inauguration in 1889. It was replaced in 1895 by a marble arch which still stands in Washington Square today.

New York City incorporates five boroughs.

Surviving the Trip

Many early immigrants sold all their possessions to pay for the ship's fare to America. The journey was long and physically arduous. 2,000 or more people traveled on each ship, and one in ten died. Many had almost no possessions or money when they arrived in New York. Today immigrants arrive on airplanes as well as ships.

Immigrants arrived in thousands on Atlantic liners.

NEW YORK CITY'S POPULATION

Only Manhattan's population is shown until 1898, when the boroughs joined the city of Greater New York. After 1898, totals for the whole city are shown. Population figures also include births, deaths, and migrants from elsewhere in America.

8,000 BC–1626 Native Americans inhabit the area. Population numbers unknown. Non-Native American populations below:

Year	Population
1624	8
1664	1,500
1698	4,937
1703	4,375
1712	5,840
1723	7,248
1790	33,131
1800	60,489
1810	96,373
1820	123,706
1830	202,589
1860	813,669
1880	1,206,299
1890	1,515,301
1900	3,437,202
1910	4,766,883
1920	5,620,048
1930	6,930,446
1940	7,454,995
1950	7,891,957
1960	7,781,984
1970	7,894,862
1980	7,071,639
1990	7,322,564
2000	8,008,278

Immigration

Right: When new immigrants first arrived in New York Bay, they saw the Statue of Liberty – the symbol of their hope for a better life in America.

The Golden Door

"Give me your tired, your poor, / Your huddled masses yearning to breathe free, / The wretched refuse of your teeming shore. / Send these, the homeless, tempest-tost, to me, / I lift my lamp beside the golden door!" EMMA LAZARUS

This poem is inscribed at the base of the Statue of Liberty.

Many immigrant families arrived in New York with only a few possessions.

New York has seen the immigration of people of all religions and cultures for over 400 years, making it one of the most multicultural cities in the world. First came the Dutch and British colonists, joined later by Scandinavians, Germans, French Protestants, Jews, and Africans brought into slavery. Great waves of immigration started in the early 1800s, as hundreds of thousands fled famine and poverty in Ireland and Germany, and continued into the 20th century as Puerto Ricans, Dominicans, and Cubans arrived. Despite tensions over the years, these varied ethnic groups have lived and worked in New York in relative peace and harmony, and are living evidence of the city's democratic ideals.

Ellis Island

New York opened its first immigration center at Castle Garden in 1855. It processed more than eight million immigrants before closing in 1892, when the federal government opened the Ellis Island complex (right). Ellis Island handled medical exams, interviews, bureaucratic records, and transportation for more than 12 million immigrants (two-thirds of the U.S. total) from 1892 to 1924. Its officials processed over 7,000 people a day. Today Ellis Island houses the American Museum of Immigration.

Health checks took place on arrival at Ellis Island.

Exams

The most frightening experience at Ellis Island was the medical exam. Doctors rejected anyone suffering from disabilities, contagious diseases, serious illnesses, or suspected insanity. Failing this exam meant automatic deportation. Polygamists, criminals, and anarchists were also rejected. Nevertheless, officials turned back fewer than two percent of all immigrants.

The novelist Henry James visited Ellis Island in 1907, and wrote of people "herded, divided, subdivided, sorted, sifted, searched, fumigated … day by day and year by year.."

Arrival in the City

After Ellis Island, immigrants traveled by ferry to Battery Park in lower Manhattan, where relatives, friends, immigrant aid workers, and aggressive con artists rushed to greet them.

Annie Moore (left), a fifteen-year-old Irish girl, was the first person to be processed at Ellis Island on January 1, 1892. She arrived on the steamship Nevada with her two younger brothers. This bronze statue of Annie stands in the Ellis Island Immigration Museum.

WAVES OF IMMIGRATION IN NEW YORK CITY

Group	Reason	Era	Approx. numbers
Jews	Fleeing persecution in Brazil	1654	30
Protestants	Fleeing persecution in France	1685	20
Africans	Brought as slaves	1626 – 1799	25,000
Irish	Escaping famine and oppression	1845 – 1860s	200,000
Germans	Escaping poverty	1850s – 1860s	150,000
Chinese	Fleeing racism in USA West	1850s – 1880	1,000
Jews	Persecution in E. Europe, Russia	1880 – 1920	1,800,000
Italians	Escaping poverty	1880s – 1910s	2,000,000
Former slaves	Escaping racism in USA South	1917	100,000
Jews	Survivors of WWII leaving Europe	1945 – 1952	85,000
Puerto Ricans	New USA citizens escaping poverty	1950s	500,000
Chinese	Escaping poverty	1980s	26,000

The Lower East Side

Most immigrants settled near familiar sights and sounds: foods from home and people who spoke and dressed as they did. Early 19th century Irish immigrants moved to the Lower East Side, where the first St. Patrick's Cathedral stood. Germans moved to Kleindeutschland ("Little Germany"), where German food shops and newspapers thrived. In the late-19th century, many Jews settled into the overcrowded Lower East Side tenements. Italians moved to Little Italy, keeping their regional loyalties: Sicilians, for example, lived on Elizabeth Street, and the Genoese on Baxter Street. Poverty, as well as familiarity, kept people in these neighborhoods until they could afford to move out.

Mulberry Street in the Lower East Side in the early 1900s.

Program for Israel Zangwill's play The Melting Pot, 1908.

The Melting Pot

"The Melting Pot" is an expression to describe the process of mixing everyone in New York together to create a single, new culture. It comes from the 1908 play by Londoner Israel Zangwill, who believed that New Yorkers would create a new, composite breed of American. Other writers, convinced that New Yorkers maintained separate cultures next to each other, compared the city to a tapestry or a mosaic.

Right: A sweatshop floor in the early 20th century.

Cultural Pride

Immigrants brought many traditions from their home countries to New York. This photo (left) shows a shrine to an Italian community's patron saint, Our Lady of Help, during a festival on Mott Street in 1908.

Americanization

Immigrants moved to America hoping for better lives for themselves and their children. The best way to get ahead was through education. In the schools, children learned English, American history, manners, good hygiene, math, and loyalty to the American Constitution and the flag.

Children took the Pledge of Allegiance in school.

Labor

Many new immigrants worked long hours in crowded factories and sweatshops (left). In 1911 a fire in the Triangle Shirtwaist factory killed 146 immigrant workers. This tragedy led to strong union labor organizations. Immigrants also worked as manual laborers, peddlers, wholesale merchants, teachers, domestic servants, bakers, waiters, newspaper-sellers, launderers, and tailors.

FESTIVALS IN NEW YORK CITY

FESTIVAL	PLACE	DATE
Chinese New Year	Chinatown	End January/Early February
St. Patrick's Day Parade	Fifth Avenue	March 17
Greek National Day Parade	Fifth Avenue	Saturday near March 25
Ukrainian Festival	E. 7th Street	Mid-to-late May
Feast of St. Anthony of Padua	Little Italy	Early-to-mid June
Puerto Rican Day Parade	Fifth Avenue	First Sunday in June
Jewish Festival	Lower E. Side	Second Sunday in June
Harlem Week	Harlem	Early-to-mid August
West Indian-American Carneval	Brooklyn	Labor Day Weekend
Feast of San Gennaro	Little Italy	Mid-September
Steuben Day Parade	Fifth Avenue	Third weekend in September
Pulaski Day Parade	Fifth Avenue	Sunday near October 5
Hispanic-American Day Parade	Fifth Avenue	Mid-October

Foods

Immigrants have made New York's cuisine the most varied in the world. New Yorkers eat burritos, felafel, dim sum, kebabs, jerk chicken, gyros, sushi, curries, blintzes, croissants, and knishes on a regular basis. America's first pizzeria, Lombardi's, was established on Spring Street in 1905 by immigrants from Naples. The Ninth Avenue International Festival in May features stands selling foods from around the world.

Neighborhoods

Some neighborhoods still reflect the cultures of the countries from which their inhabitants have come. Chinatown (left) has been one such enclave since the 1850s. Others include Little Italy, Spanish Harlem (a Hispanic community), and Little Odessa (a Russian community).

Hotdog sellers (below) are the modern equivalent of the weiner vendors who came from Germany in the 1800s. Germans in Kleindeutschland also invented New York's favorite institution, the delicatessen.

Work Today

Today many immigrants drive taxi cabs and run neighborhood grocery stores, food stands, and restaurants. They also work as caretakers, teachers, and in numerous other professions.

In the final decades of the 20th century, New York replaced Paris as the cultural hub of the Western world. It was immediately after World War II, however, that the city began to draw young artists and intellectuals in unprecedented numbers. Offering iconoclastic individuals the freedom to live as they wished, New York seemed the perfect place for the explorations of the post-war era. Along with its mood of freedom, the city's scale, pace and complex beauty also worked as a magnet and a source of inspiration.

Edith Wharton (left) wrote novels about the upper-class society around Washington Square, into which she was born in 1862. Other great New York writers include Washington Irving, Herman Melville, Henry James, and F. Scott Fitzgerald.

Jackson Pollock action painting.

Artists, Writers,

Art in the City

Before the mid-20th century, New York artists looked to Europe for inspiration. After 1945, they created their own radical new art movements, including Abstract Expressionism (1940s and 1950s), Pop Art (1960s and 1970s), and Graffiti Art (1980s). New York still dominates the modern art world, with artists congregating in various neighborhoods, such as SoHo, Chelsea, Williamsburg and Long Island City.

Abstract Expressionism

Painters Jackson Pollock (left) and Willem de Kooning led New York's first art movement, Abstract Expressionism. In the 1950s, they radicalized painting by experimenting with styles and self-expression. One outcome was Pollock's "action painting," which involved dripping paint onto a canvas on the floor.

ARTISTS, WRITERS, AND INTELLECTUALS

1638 New Amsterdam's first school is founded.

1693 The first printing press set up.

1735 Peter Zenger, publisher of the "Weekly Journal", is acquitted for libel against the Royal Governor, establishing a precedent for freedom of expression.

1754 King's College (now Columbia University) opens.

1846 The Associated Press (AP) is founded.

1877 The American

Edward Hopper painted the famous 'Nighthawks' (above).

Pop Art

Andy Warhol worked as an illustrator before becoming the leader of New York's Pop Art movement in the 1960s. Pop artists, such as Roy Lichtenstein, were fascinated by America's banal popular culture, and defiantly set out to prove that anything could be art. Warhol mass produced silk-screened images of Campbell's soup cans (left) and celebrities. A celebrity himself, Warhol famously predicted, "In the future, everyone will be famous for 15 minutes."

Andy Warhol (above) became famous for his hip New York lifestyle too.

Graffiti Art

In the 1970s and 1980s a rebellious New York subculture created urban Graffiti art – bright, elaborate works scrawled illegally in spray paint across buildings and subway cars. Graffiti art gained recognition when Stefan Eins opened a gallery in the Bronx devoted to works by Crash and other self-trained artists. Later artists include Jean-Michel Basquiat and Keith Haring, pictured right with one of his works in the background.

Ashcan School

The Ashcan School movement developed in the early 20th century in Greenwich Village, where artists used a realistic style to portray the tenements, saloons, and working-class streets of their everyday lives. John Sloan, Robert Henri, and George Bellows led the movement, but one of its best-known students is Edward Hopper. Hopper studied painting under Henri, but soon developed an independent style that conveys urban isolation and loneliness.

Museum of Natural History opens.

1880 The Metropolitan Museum of Art opens.

1895 Tne New York Public Library is founded.

1913 Armory Show introduces New Yorkers to "modern art."

1925 Harold Ross founds The New Yorker magazine.

1929 The Museum of Modern Art (MoMA) opens.

1931 The Whitney Museum of American Art opens.

1933 "Esquire" and "Newsweek" magazines begin publication.

1960 An estimated two-thirds of America's artists live and work in New York.

1962 Andy Warhol launches Pop Art.

2000 The Brooklyn Museum of Art resists mayoral pressure to close.

The Harlem Renaissance

Writers and intellectuals, including Langston Hughes (right), Marcus Garvey, and Zora Neal Hurston flocked to Harlem in the early 20th century, contributing greatly to Harlem Renaissance culture

Dorothy Parker (left) was one of the founders of the Algonquin Round Table.

(see also page 28.) In addition, the social and political atmosphere of Harlem at the time led to the foundation of the National Association for the Advancement of Colored People (NAACP).

The Algonquin Round Table

In 1919, a circle of literary and theatrical friends gathered daily for lunch at a large, round table in the Rose Room restaurant at the Algonquin Hotel, a tradition that continued until 1943. Many of these writers,

critics, and columnists, including Dorothy Parker (right) and Robert Benchley, reported the group's witty, sarcastic remarks in the press: "All the things I really like to do are either immoral, illegal, or fattening," said Alexander Woollcott.

Polly's Restaurant (below) in Greenwich Village was an enclave for writers and artists in the 1920s.

and Intellectuals

Greenwich Village

America's first genuinely bohemian enclave thrived in the lower Manhattan neighborhood of Greenwich Village in the 1910s and 1920s. Writers, artists, intellectuals, and actors gathered in tea shops, taverns, and inexpensive

restaurants like Polly's (below left) to discuss socialism, communism, anarchism, feminism, birth control, art, poetry, and theater. Famous residents included Dylan Thomas, Emma Goldman, Malcolm Cowley, Margaret Sanger, e.e. cummings, and John Dos Passos.

The Beat Generation

Poet Allen Ginsberg, a student at Columbia University, met the writer Jack Kerouac one afternoon in 1944, and together they visited the writer William Boroughs on Riverside Drive. They all became friends, and then key figures of the Beat Generation in the 1950s and 1960s.

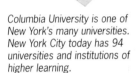

Columbia University is one of New York's many universities. New York City today has 94 universities and institutions of higher learning.

Magazines

New York City was already publishing more than 600 magazines by the 1920s, including Time, Vogue, Vanity Fair, and The New Yorker (right), which promised to be "a reflection in words and pictures of metropolitan life."

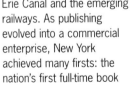

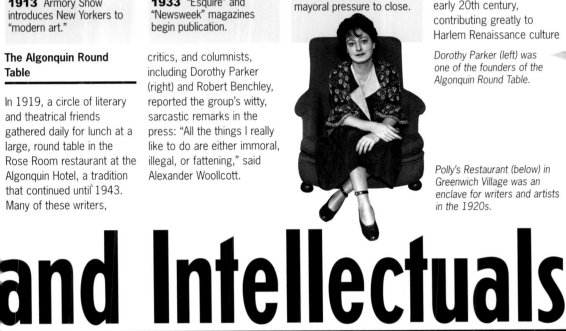

SoHo

The name SoHo (South of Houston), for the East Side neighborhood between Houston and Canal Streets, was invented in the 1960s. Rents were cheap, and artists converted many commercial buildings into artist-only cooperatives of spacious lofts. Art dealers and their galleries soon followed. Rents are now high, but SoHo is still a center of contemporary art.

One of the many art galleries in SoHo, New York.

Publishing Capital of America

In the 1850s, New York's printing presses churned out novels, newspapers, and magazines to distribute to the nation by boat on the

Erie Canal and the emerging railways. As publishing evolved into a commercial enterprise, New York achieved many firsts: the nation's first full-time book reviewer in the 1850s, the first comic book in 1904, the

first crossword puzzle in 1913, and the first Barnes and Noble bookstore in 1917. The city is still filled with avid readers, and has more than 500 bookstores.

Strand Book Store on Broadway.

New York illustrator James Montgomery Flagg used his own face to depict Uncle Sam in this famous recruitment poster (left).

Over There sold two million copies of sheet music. The lyrics went, "So prepare, say a pray'r, Send the word, send the word, to beware."

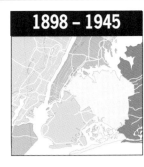

1898 – 1945

1902 The teddy bear is invented in a candy store in Brooklyn, in honor of New Yorker President Theodore Roosevelt.

1904 The first commercially successful subway opens. The New

York Times relocates to Times Square, renamed in its honor.

1911 The Triangle Shirtwaist Factory fire kills 146

1913 The Woolworth Building is the world's tallest building.

"Over There"

When America entered World War I in 1917, New Yorkers reacted with brisk patriotism. In all, 1.5 million soldiers were dispatched through New York's port and the city became America's war propaganda headquarters. James Montgomery Flagg drew his famous poster of Uncle Sam to recruit soldiers, and Broadway songwriter George M. Cohan wrote *Over There*, a patriotic song hummed by millions, including the President. When the war ended in 1918, soldiers returned to victory parades and memorial ceremonies that continued in New York for a year.

Babe Ruth hitting a home run.

Babe Ruth was one of the first sports superstars to sell his name through merchandise, like the Baby Ruth candy bar.

Greater New York

Prohibition and Crime

When alcohol was outlawed in 1920, New Yorkers set up 32,000 speakeasies, or illegal bars. Before Prohibition was repealed in 1933, this number rose to around 50,000. The most famous speakeasy was Jack and Charlie's Club at 21 West 52nd Street, known as "21." In the Prohibition era organized crime syndicates ran the alcohol trade, making the fortunes of gangsters like Charles "Lucky" Luciano (right) and Benjamin "Bugsy" Siegal.

Customers in a New York speakeasy bar.

Coney Island

Named Konijn Eiland (Rabbit Island) by the Dutch colonists, Coney Island was once the world's most famous amusement park. Between 1897 and 1904, three spectacular attractions opened: Steeplechase Park; Luna Park (left), with its 250,000 incandescent light bulbs; and Dreamland, with one million lights. Coney Island had a roller coaster, a two-mile-long boardwalk, vaudeville shows, Nathan's famous hotdogs, fortune tellers, wax museums, the Tunnel of Love boat ride, and more. In 1920 the subway connected it to Manhattan, and millions came out to play in the 1920s, 1930s, and 1940s.

LUNA PARK, SURF AVENUE, BY NIGHT, CONEY ISLAND, N. Y.

A New York street in the 1920s. People worked on the city's sidewalks, selling food or shining shoes. Children sold newspapers on the streets, shouting out the headlines to lure buyers.

1923 Yankee Stadium opens in the Bronx.

1927 The world's first television pictures broadcast from New York.

Babe Ruth

In the 1920s, New York had three major-league baseball teams: the Yankees (Bronx), the Giants (Manhattan), and the Dodgers (Brooklyn). One superstar ruled, though: George Herman "Babe" Ruth of the Yankees. Babe Ruth hit 59 home runs in 1921. In 1923, New York opened today's Yankee Stadium in the Bronx.

As New York entered the 20th century, it did so as a newly consolidated city with a population of over three million people. With its towering skyscrapers and financial strength, New York flourished as a self-confident, cosmopolitan city. Its streets were alive with a buzz of constant activity, the newly-built subway was an integral part of everyday life and, despite prohibition, music and entertainment were enjoyed everywhere. A leading port of entry for thousands of immigrants, New York's character began to take a distinctly multicultural shape, as people from all over the world came to the city, attracted by its prosperity and its gilded promises of opportunity.

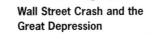

Unemployment affected thousands of people. Soup kitchens were set up to feed the long-term unemployed.

I KNOW 3 TRADES
I SPEAK 3 LANGUAGES
FOUGHT FOR 3 YEARS
HAVE 3 CHILDREN
AND NO WORK FOR
3 MONTHS
BUT I ONLY WANT
ONE JOB

October 29, 1929
The Stock Market crashes, starting the Great Depression.

1930 The Chrysler Building is the world's tallest building.

1931 The Empire State Building is the world's tallest building.

1933 Fiorello La Guardia

becomes New York's mayor, a position he holds until 1945.

1935 First Houses, the first public housing project in America, is built on the Lower East Side.

1939 President Roosevelt, at the opening of the World's Fair, becomes the first

President to appear on TV.

1940 Rockefeller Center opens. The Murder Inc. crime syndicate is exposed.

1945 Dr. Robert Oppenheimer's "Manhattan Project" atomic bomb helps to end World War II. 16,000 New Yorkers died in World War II.

As Manhattan made its way through the Roaring Twenties, more or less survived the Great Depression, and gave its all to the war effort, the outlying boroughs became ever more defined worlds of their own. People moved to Brooklyn and Queens in large numbers, and for the first time in the city's history, Manhattan was not the most populous part of New York. The onset of the Depression ended the period of tremendous growth in the outer boroughs that had begun in the 1880s, but privately funded apartment buildings and parks continued to be built. At the end of World War II the prevailing feeling was of great hope and optimism for the future.

The Roaring Twenties (right) ended abruptly with the Wall Street Crash of 1929. Many people, financially ruined, (cartoon, above) saw no alternative to ending their lives.

Wall Street Crash and the Great Depression

In the Roaring Twenties, stock market prices soared ever-higher, until investors panicked and rushed to sell

Lindbergh

Aviator Charles Lindbergh (right) made the first solo nonstop flight across the Atlantic from New York to Paris in 1927. He returned to a hero's welcome in New York City in May of that year.

their stocks. On October 29, 1929, they dumped over 16 million shares, causing the New York stock market to crash. Thousands of small investors lost their life savings, more than 100,000 lost their homes, dozens of banks went bankrupt, and

10,000 factories shut down. By 1933, a quarter of New York's population was unemployed (above left). Many waited at charitable soup kitchens for their only food (left), and lived in shacks. The Great Depression lasted until the late 1930s.

Mayor Fiorello La Guardia.

The Famous
COTTON CLUB
The Aristocrat of Harlem
142nd Street & Lenox Ave

Presents
DAN HEALY'S
NEW SPARKLING
LIGHTNING FAST
PRODUCTION

**COTTON CLUB
ON PARADE**

CAB CALLOWAY
and his famous Cotton Club orchestra

Reservations advisable   *Bradhurst 2·7767·1687*

The Harlem Renaissance

African-Americans fleeing racism in lower Manhattan and the American South moved to Harlem in the early 20th century. There they could rent decent apartments, thanks to realtor Philip A. Payton. During the 1920s, Harlem's population doubled to 200,000. Writers, artists, and intellectuals gathered

and debated in this great city-within-the-city, while the world's best blues and jazz music flowed in clubs, where Duke Ellington, Billie Holliday, Louis Armstrong, and Cab Calloway, among others, performed. Harlem dancers invented the Charleston, the turkey trot, and the boogie-woogie.

Right: Dressed to the nines on Seventh Avenue and 124th Street. In the 1920s, Harlem was famous for its elegant street life.

Cab Calloway starred at the Cotton Club (left). In many Harlem nightclubs of this era, African-Americans performed, but only white people could be patrons.

Duke Ellington's success at the Cotton Club caused its "whites only" policy to be relaxed.

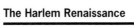

Left: The brightly lit "Great White Way" of New York City was the center of musicals and theater.

Below: The Rockettes appeared at Radio City Hall, the world's largest theater when it opened in 1932.

The huge exhibit area (above) of the World's Fair held in New York in 1939–40.

Times Square and the "Great White Way"

In 1904 the New York Times moved uptown to Longacre Square, which was renamed Times Square in the newspaper's honor. To this day its electrically-lit, moving news bulletin remains on the One Times Square building. In the 1930s and 1940s, New York's artistic and commercial power emanated from Broadway at Times Square, where the American musical was invented. F. Garcia Lorca wrote of the brightly-lit "Great White Way": "Broadway at night was breathtaking ... a magnificent, moving spectacle put on by the boldest, most modern city in the world."

The World's Fair

New York hosted the 1939–40 World's Fair in Queens, with the theme "Building the World of Tomorrow." The fair introduced 25 million visitors to television, sheer nylon stockings, and the Futurama exhibit, which envisioned America in 1960. The fair's symbols, the Trylon (a 700-foot obelisk) and the Perisphere (a 200-foot globe), appeared on the sheet music for the fair's song *Dawn of a New Day* (above left), by Pulitzer-prize-winning songwriter George Gershwin and his brother Ira. When the United States entered World War II, the steel that the Trylon and Perisphere were made of was donated to the U.S. military.

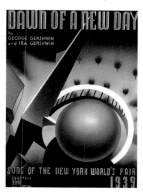

The sheet music for Dawn of a New Day, *the theme song of the World's Fair, 1939–40.*

Statue of Liberty in World War II dimout.

World War II

During World War II, lights were dimmed throughout New York City: on the Statue of Liberty; on the Empire State Building; and in Times Square (to obscure it from potential German bomber planes). Three million soldiers and 63 million tons of supplies embarked for Europe from New York Harbor, massively boosting the city's economy.

Right: When World War II ended on August 14, 1945, New Yorkers gathered in Times Square to celebrate.

Ethnic Diversity in Brooklyn

Brooklyn has played a major role in New York's long history of immigration (see Immigration, pages 22–23). It hosts communities of Jamaicans, Asians, and Guyanese, but is perhaps most noted for its enclaves of Jews and Italians, who poured into the borough at the turn of the 20th century. Parts of Bensonhurst in Brooklyn are lined with Italian cafés, bakeries, and pizzerias, while Hasidic Jews, in their black hats and flowing coats, populate many parts of the borough.

With headquarters in the borough, the ultra-Orthodox Hasidic Jews are a familiar sight on the streets of Brooklyn.

Below: This Dutch colonial farmhouse was built around 1652 by Pieter Claesen Wyckoff. Arriving from Holland as an indentured servant in 1637, he eventually became a wealthy farmer.

Prospect Park

Following the success of Central Park (see page 17), designers Olmsted and Vaux laid out Prospect Park in Brooklyn in the 1860s. With 526 acres of woods, meadows, and lakes, by the mid-1880s much of the park was set aside for lawn tennis. In the 1900s the annual May Day festival brought thousands of children into the park

The Boathouse along the Lullwater in Prospect Park was designed by Frank J. Helmle and Ulrich Huberty in 1905.

1630 The Dutch attempt colonization of Staten Island.

1636 First settlement in the Brooklyn area by Dutch farmers.

1664 The English rename the Staten Island area Richmond.

Brooklyn and

A Dutch Legacy

Before the English took over Brooklyn in 1664, the Dutch had ruled the area, naming it Breuckelen (the present spelling of the borough was fixed at the end of the 18th century). Despite their short rule, the Dutch left a significant mark on Brooklyn. Street names, churches, cemeteries, and houses all bore the marks of Dutch occupation, while the Dutch language is said to have been spoken as late as the 1880s in some parts of Brooklyn. Even today, Dutch influence is evident in street names such as New Ultrecht Avenue, while there are 14 Dutch-American farmhouses in the borough, the oldest being that of Pieter Wyckoff in the Flatlands area.

This card shows the Brooklyn Bridge, which spurred the development of Brooklyn in the late 19th century.

The largest of the boroughs, Brooklyn is the quintessential city of immigrants. One out of every seven Americans can trace their family roots through the streets of Brooklyn. Today Creole, Arabic, Spanish, Chinese, and Korean are spoken, in addition to Russian, Polish, Albanian, Italian, and Yiddish. City that it is, Brooklyn also occupies a special place in the American imagination. The Brooklyn Bridge, Coney Island, and Ebbets Field are just a few of the magical names that conjure numerous images epitomizing the American experience. In stark contrast, across the river is Staten Island, the often "forgotten borough," with its famous orange ferries and Sailors' Snug Harbor, which opened in 1833 as the first maritime home and hospital for retired seamen in America. Today Snug Harbor is a cultural center housed in 28 unusual historic buildings.

19th Century Brooklyn

Francis Guy's famous Winter Scene in Brooklyn (right), depicting the city sometime between 1817 and 1820, shows a largely rural community. People can be seen gathering wood and making deliveries, while pigs, cattle, and chickens roam the streets. By the end of the 19th century, however, Brooklyn was a very different place. Sugar refining was its largest industry, downtown Brooklyn was densely packed with commercial and manufacturing buildings, and cultural institutions, like the Brooklyn Museum, marked the beginnings of a golden period for the borough.

This U.S. postage stamp featuring the Verrazzano-Narrows Bridge was issued in 1964 to commemorate the bridge's opening.

1776 The Battle of Long Island is fought in Brooklyn.

1860 The railroad is extended along both sides of Staten Island.

1876 Over 200 people die in the Brooklyn Theatre fire.

1897 First section of the

Brooklyn Museum of Art is opened.

1900 Population of Brooklyn reaches 1,000,000. Staten Island, with 67,021 inhabitants, is the smallest of the five boroughs.

1911 The Brooklyn Botanical Garden and

Arboretum is founded.

1929 The Williamsburg Savings Bank Tower, the highest building in Brooklyn, is built.

1936 The Staten Island Zoo opens.

1951 The Brooklyn Promenade is built.

1957 The Brooklyn Dodgers play their last game at Ebbets Field. They move to Los Angeles a year later.

1965 Brooklyn Heights is designated a New York Historic District.

1975 The Borough of Richmond is renamed the

Borough of Staten Island.

1989 The Brooklyn Philharmonic is formed.

2001 79 streets on Staten Island are renamed after victims of the September 11 disaster.

Staten Island

Crossing the Bridge

Staten Island's long association with New York originated from a 17th century bet. When the British took over New Amsterdam in 1664, New Jersey claimed Staten Island as it's own. As a way

of settling the dispute, the Duke of York declared that the island would be awarded to the province whose citizen could circumnavigate it in less than a day. The bet was won for New York by Christopher Billopp, a British naval captain. For much of the 18th and early 19th

centuries, Staten Island was involved in farming, oystering, and fishing, and remained largely untouched by the immense changes in Manhattan. With the arrival of a regular ferry service to Manhattan in the 1820s, the island became less rural and industry, such as breweries and dye works, began to appear along its shoreline. The opening of the Verrazzano-Narrows Bridge in 1964 saw a growth in population on the island, but also brought an increase in crime and poverty.

Nathan's Hotdogs

Founded on Coney Island in 1916 by Nathan Handwerker, Nathan's hotdogs quickly became a Brooklyn icon. In its heyday in the 1920s and 1930s,

The original Nathan's hotdog store can still be found on Coney Island.

Coney Island (see page 26) in southern Brooklyn was packed with thrilling rides, shows, and performers. Once the subway was extended to Coney, Nathan's became world famous, with throngs of New Yorkers and tourists alike sampling its famous hotdogs.

Staten Island to Manhattan by Ferry

A municipal service since 1905, the Staten Island ferry travels between the Battery in Manhattan and St. George on Staten Island. Over the years, there have been an array of ferries with many different names, from the Knickerbocker in 1931 to

125 passengers were killed aboard the Staten Island ferryboat, Westfield II, after a boiler explosion in 1871.

the Gold Star Mother in 1937, which honored mothers who had lost their sons during World War I.

Francis Guy (1760 – 1820) is said to have painted this Brooklyn scene from his second-storey window overlooking the street.

Traditional brownstone houses line many of the streets in Brooklyn Heights.

Brooklyn Heights

An old residential neighborhood, Brooklyn Heights began to develop after 1814 when Robert Fulton's ferry service enabled people to cross the river to Manhattan. Throughout the 19th century, Brooklyn Heights was noted for its churches and fine houses, which were built in many different styles — Federal, Greek, Gothic, and Queen Anne.

QUEENS

1636 First Dutch settlement is established near Flushing Bay.

1665 Horse racing begins at Salisbury Plains.

1683 Queens county is established.

1790 First national census records 5,393 inhabitants in Queens.

1851 A law prohibiting further burials in Manhattan leads Queens to become the new resting place of many New Yorkers.

1870's William Steinway, a piano manufacturer, begins production in East Astoria.

1882 Ozone Park is created.

1884 Morris Park is created.

1909 Queensboro Bridge is constructed.

1917 Hell's Gate Bridge is opened between the Bronx and Astoria.

Catherine of Braganza, wife of King Charles II of England, after whom Queens was named in 1683.

Early Life in Queens

As in the other New York boroughs, the original inhabitants of Queens were the Native Americans, who were followed by the Dutch and English in the 17th century. During the Revolution, most residents of Queens were British sympathizers, many of whom fled at the end of the war fearing reprisals for having supported the enemy. Until the 1830s, Queens remained an area of farms and small villages, and its population hardly increased at all.

A Suburban Borough

Between 1910 and 1930 the number of New Yorkers living in Manhattan dropped considerably. Families were moving out to the boroughs, as transportation links improved and suburban housing development boomed. Real estate agents bought up acres of land in Queens and garden apartment buildings sprang up in many areas. By the 1960s, Queens was still experiencing a residential boom, as new houses were built everywhere.

An advertisement for garden apartments in Jackson Heights in 1925. Jackson Heights was the essence of suburban living with tennis courts, playgrounds, and a community center.

Queens

A rural, farming community for much of its life, Queens experienced its first population explosion in the early 20th century and another after World War II. It was in the 1930s, however, that those constructions that help to give Queens its own specific identity were first built. The Triborough Bridge and Grand Central Parkway opened in 1936, Queens College in 1937, and LaGuardia Airport in 1939. It was the World's Fair of 1939-40, however, that finally put the borough on the national map. Today Queens is a massive, multi-ethnic urban complex, home to Greeks, Italians, Japanese, Chinese, Koreans, Colombians, Asian Indians, Puerto Ricans, Jews, Maltese, and many others.

Turn of the Century Queens

Although still largely rural, mid-19th century Queens was changing. A few industries were established in the area, such as the Steinway piano factory and the Edward Smith & Co paint factory, and the first signs of urbanization appeared. By the early 20th century, it had a population of over 150,000 and with the opening of the Queensboro Bridge in 1909 and the Long Island Railroad in 1910, Queens became an easy commute from Manhattan.

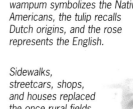

The flag of the Borough of Queens dates from 1913. The colors are those of the first Dutch governor, William Kielt. The ring of wampum symbolizes the Native Americans, the tulip recalls Dutch origins, and the rose represents the English.

Sidewalks, streetcars, shops, and houses replaced the once rural fields of Queens, as seen here in Jamaica, Queens in 1915.

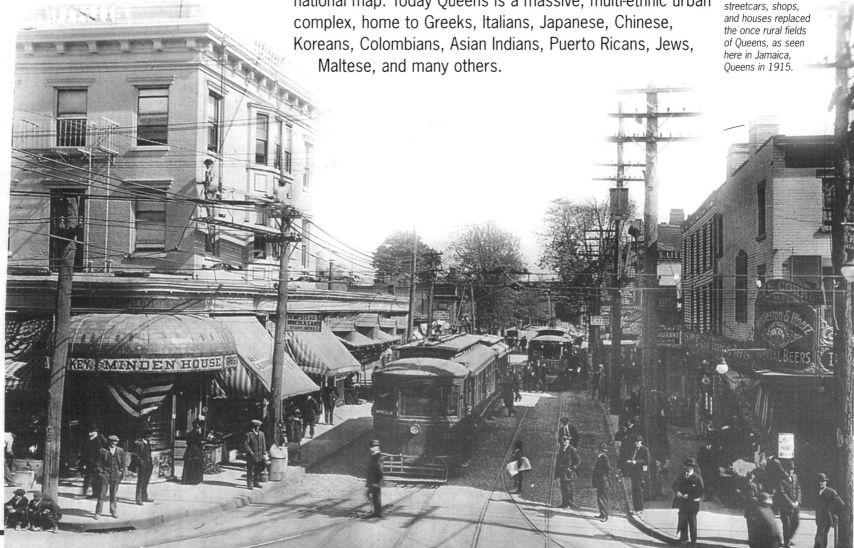

1920s Population rockets from 469,042 to 1,079,129.

1930 America's first supermarket opens on Jamaica Avenue.

1939-40 First of the two World's fairs is held in Flushing Meadows.

1964 Shea Stadium opens.

1964-65 Second World's Fair is held in Queens.

1972 The Queens Museum of Art is established.

1978 US Open Tennis Championships move to Flushing Meadow from Forest Hills.

1990 Population of Queens

reaches 1,951,598.

2001 An airplane crashes in the Rockaway area of Queens.

These young Korean immigrants are celebrating the lunar new year in Flushing, Queens by playing Korean folk drums to bring good luck to passers-by.

Art at P.S.1

Although a large number of children attended school in the 19th century, it did not become compulsory in Queens until the 1870s. Under the Democratic mayor, Patrick J. Gleason, the First Ward Primary School, P.S.1., was built in

The P.S.1. Contemporary Art Center opens in 1976.

Long Island City in the 1880s. By 1900, there were over 1,500 children enrolled in the school, a number which had declined greatly by the middle of the century. The building was closed in the 1970s, and later restored and reopened as a contemporary art center.

Rockaway Beach

Away from the main residential and industrial areas of Queens lies the Rockaway peninsula, reaching out towards Jamaica Bay. In the early 19th century, the area was an exclusive summer resort attracting the well-to-do who stayed in large hotels or in

Rockaway Beach
EXIT 17

their own mansions. With the development of the railroad, however, the Rockaway area was put within easy reach of less affluent families. Today it still attracts New Yorkers looking to relax on the beach.

The Multicultural Borough

The second most populated borough in New York, Queens is multiethnic and home to thousands of immigrants from all over the world — Greeks, Italians, Japanese, Koreans, Asian Indians, Puerto Ricans, and Chinese, to name just a few. As early as the 1830s, the borough

experienced its first wave of immigration, as Irish and Germans moved into the area. The village of Astoria experienced change too and became the city's largest Greek enclave, known as 'Little Greece' for many years. Greek restaurants and shops line the streets, clearly evident by their blue and white store fronts, while the

Greek Orthodox church of St. Demetrios has one of the largest Greek congregations outside of Greece. Over the years, however, even Astoria has diversified, with immigrants from countries such as Mexico, Russia, and Colombia as residents.

Sports in Queens

Queens hosts some of North America's most prestigious sporting events. Since 1978, the National Tennis Center in Flushing

Meadows has held the annual U.S. Open, a tennis tournament for both amateurs and professionals. In the nearby Shea Stadium, crowds gather to watch the New

York Mets, who started playing baseball in 1962, as well as the New York Jets. When a Mets player hits a homer, the Mets Magic Top Hat produces a red Big Apple in

celebration! Costing over $25 million to build, the stadium also has hosted performers such as the Beatles, who played there in 1965 and 1966.

Both J.F.K. International Airport and LaGuardia Airport are based in Queens. Opened in 1948, John F. Kennedy International Airport, originally known as New York International Airport, was re-

dedicated on December 24, 1963, following the assassination of the U.S. president that year. This poster (above) celebrated 50 years of operation at JFK.

In August 2002, the Mets celebrated their 40th anniversary by having the fans select the "All Amazin' Team".

The Arthur Ashe Stadium sees thousands of spectators gather to watch the tennis matches of the U.S. Open.

The Van Cortlandt House (left) was built in Georgian-colonial style by Frederick Van Cortlandt. It originally stood on a wheat plantation which covered much of the borough.

Black squirrels can often be seen roaming the streets and parks of the Bronx.

THE BRONX

Jerome Park, named after its founder, New York financier Leonard W. Jerome, opened in the Bronx in 1866. From the start, spring and autumn race meetings at the park were a magnet for New York's fashionable society, who picnicked beside the racetrack.

The Bronx

Living in the Bronx

Apart from clusters of factories, coalyards, and breweries, much of the Bronx remained relatively rural until the extension of the subway saw an explosion in population at the beginning of the 20th century. Irish, Germans, Jews, Italians, and Poles were among the many different ethnic groups to arrive in the borough, leading to the development of areas such as "Little Italy". Between the wars, the Bronx was a comfortable commuter zone. The Grand Concourse with its Art Deco buildings was a popular place to live. The golden age of the Bronx came to an end, however, in the 1950s. By the end of the 1970s, the Bronx had seen some of its most tense urban struggles and only today is it beginning to regain some of its old spirit.

The only borough physically joined to mainland North America, the Bronx is said to have gotten its name from Jonas Bronck, a Swedish sea captain. Arriving in 1639, he bought land along the river, which came to be called Broncks', then The Bronx River. Until the 20th century, it was a place of farms, markets, and estates. In 1904 the first subway connecting the Bronx to Manhattan was built, bringing development and hundreds of thousands from Manhattan. After World War II a long period of decline set in. In the 1990s, the Bronx entered a period of renewal and was awarded the designation "All American City," as home to people from at least 20 countries.

The streets of the Bronx are a mix of vibrant life and abandoned stretches. In summer months, Bronx residents can often be seen opening fire hydrants to keep cool!

1639 The Dutch West India Company purchases land from the Indians that now constitutes the Bronx.

1641 Jonas Bronck purchases 500 acres of land along the river.

1748 Wealthy New Yorker, Frederick Van Cortlandt builds a home in what is now the Bronx.

1840–60 Population quadruples from 5,346 to 23,593.

1841 Fordham University is established.

1861 Gas lighting is introduced into the Bronx.

1874 The western part of the Bronx is annexed by New York City.

1889 The Bronx Zoo opens.

1890 The population of the Bronx is 88,908.

1891 The New York Botanical Garden is founded.

1904 The IRT subway is extended to the Bronx under 149th Street.

1906 The Jerome Park Reservoir is opened.

1920 The population is more than 700,000.

1940 The first enclosed market is built on Arthur Avenue.

1972 The Bronx Museum of the Arts opens.

1977 President Jimmy Carter visits the Bronx. Widespread urban devastation is reported by television and newspapers.

1997 The Bronx is awarded the designation of "All American City" by the National Civic Council.

2001 The Bronxite, General Colin Powell is appointed U.S. Secretary of State.

The 'Bronx Bombers'

Yankee Stadium, home of the New York Yankees, dates back to 1923. The team quickly became known as the "Bronx Bombers" for the large number of home runs hit by its players. Stars such as Mickey Mantle, Joe DiMaggio, and Roger Maris have since passed through its gates, and in 1976 the stadium was renovated at the huge cost of $100 million.

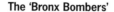

On the 50th anniversary of the opening of Yankee Stadium in 1973, Bobby Murcer and Ron Blomberg were stars of the New York Yankees.

Gorillas in the Bronx Zoo today.

Welcome to the BRONX ZOO

The Animal Kingdom

When it opened at the end of the 19th century, the Bronx Zoo had 22 exhibits and 843 animals. By 1910, the number of animals had increased to over 5,000 different specimens. In 1941, the zoo opened the African Plains, a huge moated area which allowed visitors to see animals in their natural surroundings.

Edgar Allan Poe stayed in the Bronx until 1849, but died later that year in Baltimore.

These family housing units on Lafayette Avenue in the South Bronx offer a new style of living for many residents.

Regeneration in the Bronx

Many areas of the South Bronx witnessed much social unrest in the 1970s and were widely destroyed during the 1977 blackout, which affected the whole city (see page 39). As a result, the city government built thousands of new family homes and many apartment buildings were restored in an attempt to regenerate and revitalize the area. Such was their success in rebuilding the borough's communities that in 1997 the Bronx won an "All American City" award.

Edgar Allan Poe

In 1846, Edgar Allan Poe (1809–1849), the author and poet, rented a small cottage in the Bronx in the hope that the fresh, country air would help cure his wife, Virginia, of her tuberculosis. His wife, however, died in 1847, and Poe stayed in the Bronx, where he wrote *Ulalume*, *The Bells*, and part of *Annabel Lee*. The humble cottage where he stayed now nestles among the apartment buildings of modern day Bronx.

Graffiti Art

In the early 1970s, graffiti in New York and many areas of the Bronx developed from small tags on walls to the complete spray painting of subway cars (right). Controversy mounted between those who saw the graffiti as a new and exciting art form and those who regarded it as defacement. The city authorities worked towards cleaning it up in the 1980s, as Graffiti Art (see page 24) became a new trend in modern art galleries.

Clubs

New York's many nightclubs offer every type of music imaginable. Live jazz, blues, pop, punk, rap, techno, folk, hip-hop, and salsa find enthusiastic audiences throughout the city. Nightclubs are famous for being "In" one month, and "Out" the next. New Yorkers rely on frequent nights out, friends, and reviews to keep up with developments. Many famous comedians, including Billy Crystal and Jerry Seinfeld, started out doing stand-up routines at New York's comedy clubs.

Entrance to CBGB's, one of Manhattan's most popular clubs.

ENTERTAINMENT

1624 Dutch settlers bring their favorite sport, bowling, to the new colony.

1732 New York's first theater, the New Theatre, opens on Maiden Lane.

1736 The first public concert is held at Todd's Tavern.

1798 The Park Theater opens.

1825 An Italian opera company performs Rossini's *Barber of Seville* at the Park Theater.

1835 The world's first flea circus opens on Broadway.

1845 The New York Knickerbockers play the first baseball game.

1850 A performance by "the Swedish Nightingale," singer Jenny Lind, causes a sensation.

1883 The Metropolitan Opera House opens on Broadway.

Dance

New York is home to many great dance companies. The New York City Ballet and the American Ballet Theater present classical dance at Lincoln Center. The Alvin Ailey American Dance Theater, the Brooklyn Academy of Music, the Joyce Theater, and the Martha Graham Center present modern dance. New Yorkers can learn tango, salsa, ballet, tap, soft shoe, mambo, bolero, samba, modern, ballroom, and other dances in the city's many dancing schools, and take to the floor at more than 400 venues.

Dancers from the New York City Ballet.

The Big Apple

New York City or "The Big Apple" is renowned as the biggest and best place to play or perform, and is the center of the American entertainment world. Artists as varied as rock star Jimi Hendrix, modern dance choreographer Martha Graham, and songwriter Irving Berlin were all discovered in New York. Not only is the city famous for its Broadway theaters, opera, orchestras, and ballet, but it also boasts an array of sports teams, elegant shops, and restaurants. Entertainment in New York is widespread and varied and all around the city people can enjoy concerts, nightclubs, cinemas, theaters, and the many street performers.

The Theater District

The heart of New York's theater district is in Shubert Alley, between Broadway and Eighth Avenue, and West 44th and 45th Streets. Broadway, as the theater district has come to be known, developed in the early 20th century around Times Square. Actors, agents, and producers thronged the district's restaurants, hotels, and clubs during its heyday in the 1920s. Its most recent revival has been driven by the Walt Disney Corporation, which has staged blockbuster musicals such as *The Lion King*.

Performing and Recording Music

For decades, the heart of America's music publishing business was Tin Pan Alley — 28th Street between Sixth Avenue and Broadway—where New York's biggest publishers had their offices, and the noise of songwriters pitching their new works was compared to "the crash of tin pans."

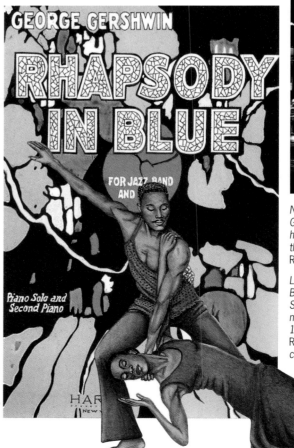

New York songwriter George Gershwin enthralled his audience in 1924 with the first performance of Rhapsody in Blue.

Left: Composer Leonard Bernstein and lyricist Stephen Sondheim created the Broadway musical West Side Story in 1956. It set Shakespeare's Romeo and Juliet in contemporary New York.

Opposite: Delmonico's Restaurant remains popular today.

Left: Some excellent music can be heard on the streets of New York.

Modern dancers from the Alvin Ailey American Dance Theater.

1914 The Strand Theater nickelodeon, the first motion picture theater, opens in New York.

1931 The Whitney Museum of American Art opens.

1932 The nation's largest indoor theater, Radio City Music Hall, opens.

1946 The New York City Ballet first performs.

1949 The opening of Arthur Miller's *Death of a Salesman* on Broadway.

1962 Avery Fisher Hall opens in Lincoln Center for the Performing Arts.

1976 To celebrate the U.S. bicentennial, the New York Marathon moved from Central Park to the streets of the five boroughs.

1997 *Cats* sets an all-time Broadway record with its 6,138th performance.

R.H. Macy & Co ("Macy's"), founded in 1858, is today the world's largest store. Its annual Thanksgiving Parade was started in 1924 as the Macy's Christmas Parade. The first giant balloons were introduced in 1927.

Shopping

As the center of America's fashion industry, New York hosts influential fashion shows twice a year. The city also is famous for its array of fancy and avant-garde boutiques, its thrift shops, and its department stores, with their innovative window displays. As Holly Golightly says in *Breakfast at Tiffany's*, "Doncha just love it?"

Some of the many fashion billboards in New York's shopping streets.

Television and Radio Broadcasting

New York's radio shows broadcast nationwide. The city has stations devoted to news, funk, soul, disco, hip-hop, rock and roll, jazz, classical, and salsa music. In 1938, Orson Wells terrified America with H.G. Wells's story *War of the Worlds* on CBS Radio. His fake news broadcast of a Martian invasion fooled millions into thinking that aliens had landed in New Jersey. The world's first television images were broadcast from New York to Washington DC, and the first commercial television station, W2XBS, opened shortly afterward in 1931.

Lincoln Center

Lincoln Center for the Performing Arts (above) includes the New York Philharmonic, the Metropolitan Opera, the New York City Opera, the New York City Ballet, and the Juilliard School of the Arts. Built between 1959 and 1969, its three largest halls—the Metropolitan Opera House, Avery Fisher Hall, and the New York State Theater – face the central plaza.

Restaurants

There are more than 15,000 restaurants in New York, offering every imaginable type of cuisine. The Russian Tea Room served blinis and borscht for more than 60 years to celebrities such as Woody Allen, who included it in his films *Manhattan* (1979) and *New York Stories* (1989). Delmonico's Restaurant (left), which opened in 1827, was one of the first to offer foreign food. For decades, it was the place to "see and be seen in New York," feeding many of the famous, such as Mark Twain.

Sports

New York sports have had a cast of memorable and outspoken characters: the left-handed home-run hitter Babe Ruth, quick-tempered tennis ace John McEnroe (left), and football star Joe Namath. Madison Square Garden is home to the celebrated New York Knicks basketball team and is where international boxing matches are held.

Yankee Stadium is home to the legendary New York Yankees. The Jets (football), Giants (football), and Rangers (ice hockey) all have fiercely loyal fans in the city.

New York Yankee's team logo.

1945 – 2002

The UN building was lit up in 1995 to celebrate its 50th anniversary.

1947 New York becomes the site of the permanent United Nations headquarters.

United Nations Headquarters

John D. Rockefeller, Jr. donated $8.5 million to the UN so that it could buy land for its base in Manhattan's Turtle Bay area. He said, "New York is a center where people from all lands have

1952 Lever House, Manhattan's first "glass-box" commercial skyscraper, opens.

1959 Frank Lloyd Wright's Guggenheim Museum building opens. *Robert Moses (right) was a dominant figure in the construction of buildings such as the Lincoln Center and the United Nations headquarters.*

always been welcomed and where they have shared common aspirations and achievements," so it was perfect for the new organization. The UN Headquarters, though located in New York, is an independent, international territory.

Urban Planning

Robert Moses (right) controlled much of the urban planning in Greater New York from 1924 until 1968, under five different mayors. He acquired enormous power through public authorities but never held an elected office. Moses envisioned and built 7 bridges, 16 expressways, and 416 miles of parkways,

shaping the modern landscape of the entire city. His legacy, however, is tainted by his racism. For example, 253 of his 255 playgrounds were in white neighborhoods. Additionally, to build his projects, he evicted hundreds of thousands from their homes, and destroyed neighborhoods. Thus, for both good and ill, the New York City of today is to a great extent the product of his vision.

1945 to the

Jackie Robinson

Jackie Robinson joined the Brooklyn Dodgers in 1947, becoming the first African-American to play in a major league. Robinson became 1947's National League Rookie of the Year, led the Dodgers in the World Series, and entered baseball's Hall of Fame.

Jackie Robinson with his 2-year-old son (Jr.) in 1949.

Puerto Rican New Yorkers

After World War II, large numbers of Puerto Ricans were drawn to the US in search of work. Today there are about one million people of Puerto Rican ancestry living in New York City. They celebrate each year with the Puerto Rican Day Parade, which an average of three million people attend.

Large crowds at the Puerto Rican Day Parade in New York.

New York emerged from World War II as the economic and cultural capital of the world. As such it was the obvious choice for the home of the United Nations. The city's post-war economic expansion brought enormous skyscrapers, world-class museums, corporate headquarters, and widespread influence. In the 1960s, Malcolm X spoke out for African-Americans in Harlem, and riots in Greenwich Village inspired a worldwide gay rights movement. By the 1970s, New York was nearing bankruptcy and crime had frightened many taxpayers away from this "urban nightmare." Recovery and an economic boom followed in the 1980s, an era of flashy materialism, but so too did widespread homelessness. The tough 1990s campaign to "clean up" the city met with both success and resentment.

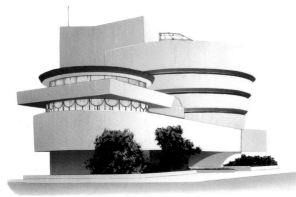

The Guggenheim Museum

Frank Lloyd Wright's architectural masterpiece, the Solomon R. Guggenheim Museum (above) opened on Fifth Avenue and 88th Street in 1959. Inside, a quarter-mile-long circular ramp rises toward a central skylight.

Along the outer walls hang works by Vincent van Gogh, Paul Klee, Andy Warhol, and many other famous artists. Wright called his building "organic architecture," because it imitates forms in nature. Critics have compared it to a snail.

1962 Philarmonic Hall (now Avery Fisher Hall) opens at the Lincoln Center.

1964 The World's Fair opens in Queens.

1965 Malcolm X is assassinated in Harlem.

1969 Gay activists riot in Greenwich Village.

1970 The first New York City Marathon takes place.

1973 The World Trade Center's Twin Towers open.

1975 13,000 fires burn in 12 square miles of the Bronx.

1977 The trend-setting disco Studio 54 opens.

The Second World's Fair

New York's second World Fair opened on April 22, 1964. Despite years of preparation, mainly under Robert Moses's direction, it was not the success its 1939 predecessor had been. It was devoted in large part to the nation's technological progress. The NASA exhibit featured full-size models of the Mercury and Apollo spacecraft.

The Unisphere of the 1964 World's Fair was on show at Flushing Meadow in Queens.

Present

During the blackout (above) of July 1977, looters, young and old, raided supermarkets and stores. Police arrested thousands of looters throughout the city.

Blackout and Crime

On July 13, 1977, lightning struck electrical power lines in Westchester County, and New York City was plunged into darkness for 25 hours. Thousands of people looted and set fires in the streets, causing $150 million of damage. Reports on this event convinced many Americans that New York was a dangerous place. This impression was confirmed over the next decade as the Mob, the mass murderer Son of Sam, and the crack cocaine epidemic hit the city. New York's dangers decreased in the 1990s, as an economic boom, a decline in crack use, and tougher policing policies helped "clean up" the city.

Near Bankruptcy

New York City almost went bankrupt in 1975, after years of inflation, the departure of the middle class (and their taxes), bad accounting practices, and cuts in federal funding. The mayor appealed to President Gerald Ford (above left), who refused to bail out the city. The Daily News reported this with the famous headline, "Ford to City: Drop Dead." So New York found other solutions: it ceded control to a watchdog agency, the Municipal Assistance Corporation; negotiated for some long-term federal aid; and slowly recovered as service industries (like publishing and finance) replaced traditional manufacturing.

An anti-war demonstration in Central Park in April 1967.

Right: Former Mayor Ed Koch was known for his aptitude in dealing with the city's financial problems.

"How'm I doing?"

Jaunty and outspoken, Ed Koch became New York's mayor in 1977, and enthusiastically cheered on the city as it entered the 1980s economic boom. Koch's city hall did everything it could to encourage the business community, and foreign investment in New York made the turn-around a huge success. Koch liked to ask New Yorkers "How'm I doing?" However Ed Koch was doing, the city was doing just fine.

Riots and Social Change

In the late 1960s and 1970s, young people across America demonstrated for women's rights, African-American rights, and an end to the Vietnam War. In New York, students at Columbia University occupied faculty offices, and demonstrators marched for peace down Fifth Avenue. The radical African-American leader Malcolm X was active in Harlem, where he was assassinated in 1965. When police raided the gay bar, the Stonewall Inn, in Greenwich Village in 1969, patrons rioted, and started the gay rights movement.

Broadway continued to produce a stream of hit musicals and plays. Andrew Lloyd Webber's musical Cats dazzled audiences when it opened in New York in October 1982. It became Broadway's longest running show, with 7,485 performances being given over a period of 18 years.

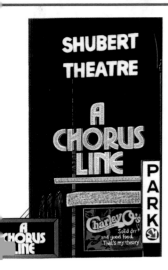

SHUBERT
THEATRE

A CHORUS LINE

PARK

A Chorus Line closed in 1990 after 6,137 performances.

David Letterman interviews President George W. Bush on the Late Show.

Rap music remains popular in New York.

Culture from the Streets

New York City's urban culture has set many trends for America, and the rest of the world. Rap music emerged on the city's streets in the 1970s, and vibrant graffiti, sprayed onto buildings, subways, and walls throughout the city, started the Graffiti art movement in the 1980s (see page 24). Today the city's fashions, hairstyles, music, dances, and slang are copied by people everywhere.

The New Millennium

The annual New Year's Eve celebration in Times Square, started in 1904, culminated in a spectacular fireworks display on December 31, 1999. More than two million people gathered in the square, and an estimated two billion people worldwide watched the celebration on television. A new, glittering, crystal ball lit by 696 lights dropped from the top of the Times Tower on the stroke of midnight, as the city of the future ushered in the new millennium.

1983 *A Chorus Line* sets a record with its 3,389th performance. "Antisliver" Law bans skyscrapers narrower than 45 feet.

1985 Hero/villain Bernhard Goetz shoots four teenagers on the subway. Murders rise as crack cocaine spreads.

1986 The 100th anniversary of the Statue of Liberty is celebrated

1990 Ellis Island reopens as a museum of immigration.

1993 A bomb at the World Trade Center causes six deaths and 1,000 injuries.

December 31, 1999 More than two million people see in the new millennium in Times Square.

2000 New York's population reaches 8,008,278.

2001 A terrorist attack on the World Trade Center kills thousands.

Late Night

New York's image as the center of American culture and nightlife was enhanced across the country by TV shows like *Late Night with David Letterman*, first broadcast in 1982 from NBC studios in the Rockefeller Center. Now *The Late Show with David Letterman* (for CBS from the Ed Sullivan Theater on Broadway), still presents Letterman in front of a fake Manhattan skyline.

Stars from the film Bonfire of the Vanities *(above) that depicted 1980s materialism. In 1987 a stock market crisis hit Wall Street (below).*

A VICTORY FOR MUGGERS!
NEW YORK POST
CRASH!
Wall Street's blackest day rocks nation
...but no 'blood in the streets'

Fans in New York mourn the death of John Lennon (above) in 1980. John Lennon was shot dead outside his home in the Dakota Apartments on December 8, 1980.

Cold, Hard Cash

The economic boom of the 1980s created many instant fortunes for New York stockbrokers and bankers, and led to a culture of self-promoting, youthful, flashy materialism. Contemporary artists, such as "neoexpressionist" Julian Schnabel, thrived in New York's SoHo, as Wall Street money bankrolled them. Writer Tom Wolfe portrayed 1980s culture in his book *Bonfire of the Vanities*. On

In the 1980s, poverty and homelessness were widespread on New York streets, as capitalism hit both extremes.

October 19, 1987, the New York Stock Market crashed, and $870 billion vanished, ending an era of conspicuous consumption.

HELP STOP HOMELESSNESS

American fashion designer Ralph Lauren with models at the end of a fashion show.

Fashion Capital

The fashion industry in New York generates sales worth more than $14 billion each year. Over 100,000 people are employed in the industry, many of them newly-arrived immigrants. New York also has eight schools dedicated to fashion, including the Fashion Institute of Technology which, with its 11,000 students, is the world's largest school of fashion.

The Times Square celebrations on December 31, 1999.

The Twin Towers

Opened in 1973, the World Trade Center was designed by Minoru Yamasaki and owned by the Port Authority of New York and New Jersey. In 1973, the Twin Towers were the tallest buildings in the world. Each tower had 104 passenger elevators and roughly an acre of rentable space on each floor. They housed more than 430 companies from 28 countries.

The Twin Towers of the World Trade Center dominated the Manhattan skyline.

The Twin Towers moments after the second airplane hit the South Tower.

The Attack

Four airplanes were hijacked on September 11. One crashed into the North Tower of the World Trade Center at 8.50 a.m., and another crashed into the South Tower at 9.04 a.m. The South Tower was the first to collapse. The North Tower followed some 30 minutes later. In separate attacks, the Pentagon building in Washington D.C. was hit by another airliner and a fourth plane crashed in a field in Pennsylvania.

The Tribute in Light on the six-month anniversary of the attack.

September 11

Rescue Services

Rescue workers toiled around the clock to save lives. New York's firefighters rushed to the scene minutes after the first plane had struck the North Tower. A command center was set up in the building's lobby as firefighters climbed the stairs. When the towers collapsed, many were trapped within and more than 300 firefighters lost their lives. Many New York City and Port Authority police were also killed in the collapse of the towers.

Life in New York City ground to a terrifying halt on the morning of September 11, 2001, when two airplanes hijacked by terrorists were flown into the Twin Towers of the World Trade Center. Disbelief turned to horror as both towers collapsed, killing almost 3,000 people. This single event took New York into a new era, as the city realized that its very openness left it vulnerable to such large-scale attack by terrorists.

The Aftermath

Ground Zero continued to burn for three months after September 11. The United States government announced its intention to wage war against terrorism.

The first target was the Taliban government in Afghanistan because of its refusal to hand over Osama bin Laden, the prime suspect in the World Trade Center attack. Across the world, memorial services took place, and a Concert for New York City raised more than $14 million to aid the families of the attack. Six months after the event two enormous beams of light paid tribute to the lost towers.

Rescue workers at "Ground Zero."

Ground Zero

The area surrounding the World Trade Center was the site of the greatest number of casualties and physical destruction. In the ensuing days, this area came to be known as "Ground Zero." A viewing platform was set up to allow visitors to pay their respects. After many months, the site finally was cleared and plans for future use of the area started to be considered .

FIDELIS AD MORTEM

Around the city people searched for loved ones by posting messages and photos in store windows and on walls and fences.

In *Here is New York*, E.B. White described New York as "the poem whose magic is comprehensible to millions of permanent residents—but whose full meaning will always remain elusive." Undaunted by this fact, many people have tried to capture the city in one sharp image or description. Many of those images and names have become part of New York's identity and allure, but none could ever embody or explain the kinetic, ever-changing city that is New York.

WHAT'S IN A NAME?

Pre-history MANNA-HATTA – The Native American name for what became Manhattan, meaning "hilly island."

1624 NEW AMSTERDAM – after the capital city of the Netherlands.

1664 NEW YORK – after the Duke of York, brother to British King Charles II.

1807 GOTHAM – from Washington Irving's satirical essays, after an English town of foolish citizens.

1825 THE EMPIRE CITY – for the city's new position at the heart of commerce.

1898 GREATER NEW YORK – a name for the incorporated five boroughs.

1908 THE MELTING POT – after an Israel Zangwill play about fusing cultures.

1926 METROPOLIS – after a Fritz Lang film about futuristic class warfare.

1930s THE BIG APPLE – called the biggest, juiciest gig on the tree of success by jazz musicians.

1931 THE WONDER CITY – from a book by W. Parker Chase, New York, "The Wonder City," but in common usage before its 1931 publication.

Gotham

Writer Washington Irving first called New York "Gotham" in 1807. He took the name from an English village that was known for its foolish citizens. However, some Gothamites only pretended to be stupid in order to trick outsiders. In 1809, Irving decided to give the new city some legends of its own, and wrote *A History of New York From the Beginning of the World to the End of the Dutch Dynasty* under the name Diedrich Knickerbocker. The name of this hilarious saga's narrator, Knickerbocker, was adopted by the New York basketball team, the Knicks.

Diedrich Knickerbocker in a 19th century illustration.

New York, New York

Metropolis

The word "metropolis" comes from Greek, and means the chief city of a country or region. New York became a real metropolis after the Erie Canal opened in 1825 (see page 16). The film *Metropolis*, by German filmmaker Fritz Lang, was inspired by his 1924 visit to New York. *Metropolis* portrays a futuristic New York City sharply divided between exploited workers living underground, and their bosses in luxurious skyscrapers. The name "metropolis" has also been applied (with more positive connotations) to the Metropolitan Museum of Art and the Metropolitan Opera.

Superman's Metropolis

The comic book hero Superman defends the city of Metropolis, which is a cleaner, sunnier, happier image of New York than Batman's gloomy Gotham. The name of the newspaper where Clark Kent works, the Daily Planet, conveys his city's importance.

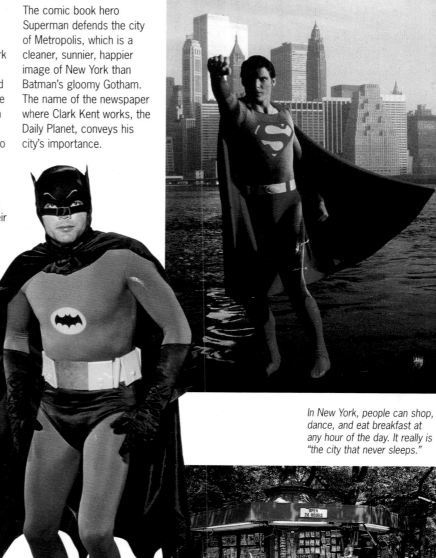

Batman's Gotham

Since 1939, the comic book superhero Batman (right) has fought crime in the dangerous city of Gotham. Batman's Gotham is a dark, brooding city with crime-riddled streets that huddle in the shadows cast by towering skyscrapers.

In New York, people can shop, dance, and eat breakfast at any hour of the day. It really is "the city that never sleeps."

Consolidation Number.

1979 THE CITY THAT NEVER SLEEPS – as in the Frank Sinatra hit, *New York, New York.*

Right: Frank Sinatra performed live in New York many times.
The Brooklyn Daily Eagle, Consolidation Issue.

New York, New York

New York, New York was singer Frank Sinatra's most popular anthem. The 1979 song tells what The Big Apple means to many people from smaller towns:

I want to wake up in a city that never sleeps

The Empire City

In the bustling years after the opening of the Erie Canal, New York's admirers called it "the Queen of American Cities," "the Great Emporium," and — the name that stuck — "the Empire City." The Empire

The John Bachmann etching of 1859 shows New York and its environs at the center of the globe.

And find I'm a number one, top of the list
These little town blues are melting away
I'll make a brand new start of it in old New York
If I can make it there, I'll make it anywhere
It's up to you, New York, New York, New York

State Building's grandeur shows what the term meant. John Bachmann's 1859 etching (left) shows the Empire City at the center of the world. Many New Yorkers then and now would agree with this view.

"Who does not know that our city is the great place of the western continent – the heart, the brain, the focus, the main spring, the pinnacle, the extremity, the no more beyond of the New World?"

WALT WHITMAN, 1842.

Left: The Wonder City of the World, 1926.

Greater New York

Greater New York describes the five boroughs — Manhattan, Brooklyn, the Bronx, Staten Island, and Queens — consolidated into one vast city in 1898. The Brooklyn Daily Eagle's editors celebrated the consolidation with this image (above) of five women joining their torches to form one brilliant flame.

The Wonder City

The self-made impresario W. Parker Chase was not the first person to call New York "The Wonder City," but he popularized the term in 1931 by publishing *New York, The Wonder City,* an imaginative guidebook to

The Big Apple

Jazz musicians in the 1930s respectfully called New York City — the biggest gig on the tree of success — The Big Apple. People liked the name so much that the New

Left: Audrey Hepburn plays the self-invented New York socialite Holly Golightly in the 1961 film Breakfast at Tiffany's. In this film she admires the luxurious displays in the windows of Tiffany & Co's store on Fifth Avenue.

NEW YORK
The WONDER CITY of the WORLD

York Convention and Visitors Bureau used it in 1971 to launch an advertising campaign that would attract visitors and make New Yorkers proud.

The Brooklyn-born filmmaker and comedian Woody Allen has set many films in New York City, including Manhattan, Annie Hall (seen below with co-star Diane Keaton in a scene from the film), and Manhattan Murder Mystery. Many Woody Allen films portray sophisticated, fast-talking, anxious New Yorkers.

the city's future. The Wonder City reflected the admiration and awe people felt when they saw New York's glowing lights, towering new skyscrapers, and brilliant entertainment.

The famous Big Apple promotional logo.

The writer, director, and actor Spike Lee (above) graduated from New York University's Film School. He shot Do The Right Thing (1989), Jungle Fever (1991), and Malcolm X (1992) on location in New York. His films comment on racial issues, class, and social behavior in the city.

"New York, indeed, resembles a magic cauldron. Those cast into it are born again".
CHARLES WHIBLEY.

Index